C   DAY
A Century of History

Dereen Taylor & Patience Coster

Evans

ON THIS DAY

A Century of History

A journey through 100 years in 365 days

First published 2008 by
Evans Brothers Limited
2A Portman Mansions
Chiltern St
London W1U 6NR

Evans celebrate 100 years of publishing in 2008 with a special centenary list, including this title.

British Library Cataloguing in Publication Data
Taylor, Dereen
   On this day: 100 years of history in 365 days
   1. History, Modern - 20th century - Miscellanea
   I. Title II. Coster, Patience
   909.8'2

ISBN-13: 9780237535285

Printed in Great Britain by Mackays of Chatham plc, Chatham, Kent

Contents

January

1

1912 THE REPUBLIC OF CHINA IS CREATED, ENDING 2,000 YEARS OF DYNASTIC RULE IN IMPERIAL CHINA BY THE QING DYNASTY.
The end of imperial rule was forced by countrywide famine in 1911, and dissatisfaction among the middle classes with China's slow rate of progress in modernising.

The last emperor, P'u Yi, stepped down from the Dragon Throne of the Manchus. The edict of abdication that was issued said:

'Today the people of the whole empire have their minds bent on a republic, the southern provinces having begun the movement, and the northern generals having subsequently supported it. The will of providence is clear and the people's wishes are plain. How could I, for the glory and honour of one family, oppose the wishes of teeming millions? Wherefore I decide that the form of government in China shall be a constitutional republic.'

After the end of imperial rule China went through periods of warlordism, Japanese invasion and civil war between the Kuomintang and the Communists, before the Communists under Mao Zedong finally secured control of the country in 1949.

1925 The US astronomer Edwin Hubble announces the discovery of galaxies outside the Milky Way.

1973 Britain, Ireland and Denmark join the European Economic Community (EEC).

2

1959 THE FIRST ARTIFICIAL SATELLITE TO GO NEAR THE MOON, *LUNA 1*, IS LAUNCHED BY THE USSR.
The satellite discovered that the Moon has no magnetic field. After passing the Moon *Luna 1* went into orbit around the Sun, between the Earth and Mars, where it has remained ever since. The Soviet lunar programme had 20 successful missions to the Moon and achieved a number of notable lunar 'firsts': first probe to impact the Moon; first flyby and image of the far side of the Moon; first soft landing; first lunar orbiter; and the first circumlunar probe to return to Earth.

3

1922 HOWARD CARTER DISCOVERS THE TOMB OF TUTANKHAMEN IN THE VALLEY OF THE KINGS, EYGPT.
The almost undisturbed tomb contained treasures of fabulous beauty and richness, sparking a worldwide interest in ancient Eygpt. A wealthy amateur, Lord Carnarvon,

had funded the work. Carter made the famous 'tiny breach in the top left-hand corner' of the doorway, and was able to peer into the tomb by the light of a candle and see that many of the young pharaoh's gold and ebony treasures were still in place. When Carnarvon asked him if he saw anything, Carter replied: 'Yes, wonderful things.'

4

1967 DONALD CAMPBELL DIES DURING A WORLD WATER SPEED RECORD ATTEMPT.
Campbell had previously set seven world water speed records, and was trying to go beyond 483 km/h (300 mph). On the second attempt, his jet-powered boat, *Bluebird K7*, flipped over at 515 km/h (320 mph), killing him instantly. His body was not discovered until 2001 – 34 years after his death.

Donald Campbell is still the only person to hold both land and water speed records at the same time.

1958 Sir Edmund Hillary becomes the first man to reach the South Pole since Captain Robert Falcon Scott's ill-fated expedition in 1912.

5

1976 CAMBODIA IS RENAMED DEMOCRATIC KAMPUCHEA BY THE KHMER ROUGE.
The brutal left-wing Khmer Rouge ruled Cambodia for four years, and in that time killed an estimated 1.5 million people out of a population of 7.5 million. In an attempt to convert the population into 'New People', its members closed schools, hospitals and factories, relocated people from towns and cities to the countryside to work on farms, abolished banking finance and currency, outlawed religion, confiscated all private property and killed anyone suspected of being an intellectual (including anyone who wore glasses). Family members that attempted to communicate with one another were also put to death.

The Khmer Rouge was driven from power by Vietnamese forces in 1979.

6

1929 MOTHER TERESA STARTS WORK IN CALCUTTA.
Born Agnes Bojaxhiu in Albania in 1910 (then part of the Ottoman Empire), Mother Teresa arrived in Calcutta to begin ministering to the poor and sick. She founded the Missionaries of Charity order, which later expanded to many other countries. The main work of the order was to provide care and compassion for the dying, allowing them dignity in their final moments.

In 1979 Mother Teresa was awarded the Nobel Peace Prize. She died in 1997.

1912 New Mexico becomes the 47th US state.

7

1989 EMPEROR HIROHITO OF JAPAN DIES.
Hirohito was the 124th emperor, reigning from 1926 until his death. Largely a figurehead politically, the emperor was worshipped as a deity, a sacred symbol and embodiment of Japan. After the end of the Second World War he was forced to deny he was a deity, but was allowed to maintain his position – the only leader of the defeated Axis powers to do so.

8

1996 FRANCE'S FORMER PRESIDENT, FRANÇOIS MITTERRAND DIES.
François Mitterrand, France's longest-serving president was a controversial figure. In 1940 he was taken prisoner after the fall of France during the Second World War. He escaped from Germany in 1941 to join the collaborationist Vichy government, and then switched allegiances to the Resistance movement. In 1971 he became leader of a new Socialist Party consisting of various disparate left-wing groups. Finally he won the presidential elections in 1981 to become the first socialist president in France in 35 years.

1912 The African National Congress is founded.

1916 Allied forces withdraw from Gallipoli after failing to defeat Turkish forces during the First World War.

9

1951 THE UNITED NATIONS HEADQUARTERS IN NEW YORK OPENS.
The United Nations (UN) was founded in 1945 to replace the League of Nations, in the hope that it would intervene in conflicts between nations and thereby avoid war. Although it is in New York City, the land occupied by the United Nations Headquarters is considered international. The organisation began with 50 countries signing the United Nations Charter. There are currently 192 members.
    The UN's most visible public figure is the secretary-general. The current secretary-general is Ban Ki-moon of South Korea, who assumed the post in January 2007.

10

1957 HAROLD MACMILLAN BECOMES CONSERVATIVE PRIME MINISTER OF BRITAIN.
Macmillan served as prime minister until 1963, when he resigned and was succeeded by Alec Douglas-Home. Macmillan will be remembered for his 'Winds of Change' speech in Cape Town, South Africa, in 1960, when he distanced himself from apartheid. His greatest achievement came in 1963, when he was heavily involved in negotiating the Nuclear Test Ban Treaty following the Cuban missile crisis.

11

1963 THE BEATLES GET THEIR FIRST UK NO. 1 HIT SINGLE – 'PLEASE, PLEASE ME'.

The Beatles – John Lennon, Paul McCartney, George Harrison and Ringo Starr – went on to become the most commercially successful and critically acclaimed band in the history of popular music. They released more than 40 No. 1 singles, albums and EPs. This commercial success was repeated around the world, with their record company, EMI, estimating that by 1985 they had sold more than one billion discs and tapes worldwide. Their innovative music and cultural impact helped define the 1960s, and their influence on pop culture can still be felt today.

1928 English novelist Thomas Hardy dies.

12

1976 CRIME WRITER AGATHA CHRISTIE DIES.

Agatha Christie was born Lady Agatha Mallowan in Oxford, England in 1890. Known as the 'Queen of Crime', Christie wrote 66 detective novels, and created two world-famous detectives, Hercule Poirot and Miss Jane Marple. An estimated one billion copies of her novels have been sold in English and she is widely considered to be one of the most important and innovative writers in the crime-fiction genre. Many of her books have been adapted for television, film and radio, including the famous *Murder on the Orient Express* and *Death on the Nile*.

Christie's stage play, *The Mousetrap*, holds the record for the longest run ever in London, opening in 1952 and still running, with more than 20,000 performances.

10

13

1930 NOVELIST JAMES JOYCE DIES.

James Joyce was born in Dublin, Ireland in 1882, the eldest of 10 children in a Roman Catholic family. In 1916, his semi-autobiographical novel *A Portrait of the Artist as a Young Man* was published, but it was the release of the landmark novel *Ulysses* in 1922 that established Joyce as one of the most influential authors of the twentieth century. Much of Joyce's work explores the issues of exile and conflict through the character widely perceived as his fictional alter-ego, Stephen Dedalus.

The life and work of James Joyce is celebrated annually on 16 June in Dublin, Ireland.

14

2005 US PRESIDENT GEORGE W. BUSH ANNOUNCES THE VISION FOR SPACE EXPLORATION PROGRAMME.

The Vision for Space Exploration programme was widely seen as an attempt to reignite enthusiasm for space travel in the US following the Space Shuttle *Columbia* disaster in 2003. The shuttle had disintegrated during re-entry into the Earth's atmosphere, killing all seven crew.

Aims of the programme include completing the International Space Station (ISS), a collaborative research facility in space, as well as exploring the Moon and Mars with robotic and crewed missions.

15

1973 US PRESIDENT RICHARD NIXON ORDERS A CEASEFIRE IN VIETNAM FOLLOWING PEACE TALKS IN PARIS.

Representatives from North and South Vietnam and the United States were involved in the negotiations, and the ceasefire finally took effect on 27 January. The settlement called for the eventual reunification of Vietnam. It permitted the South Vietnamese and Vietcong troops to remain in place and provided for the release of all American prisoners of war within 60 days, on condition American troops withdrew within the same period of time.

The settlement marked the end of American involvement in the Vietnam War, which had begun on 12 February 1955. According to American statistics from the US Defense Department, 45,933 Americans were killed in action, 181,483 South Vietnam armed forces, 5,224 foreign allies and 922,290 North Vietnamese and Vietcong.

Vietnam was finally reunited on 30 April 1975.

16

2001 AN OIL-TANKER SPILLAGE THREATENS ECO-PARADISE IN THE GALAPAGOS ISLANDS IN THE PACIFIC OCEAN.

A fuel supply tanker ran aground off the island of San Cristobal, endangering the Archipelago, almost 97 per cent of which is an Ecuadorian national park, and home to thousands of unique animal and plant species. Its tourism generates over $100 million a year for the impoverished South American country.

The ship ran aground carrying a cargo of thousands of gallons of diesel and heavy oil, and 680,000 litres (180,000 gallons) of fuel escaped into the water. Despite a large-scale clean-up operation, a June 2002 report found the effects had been very damaging to the area's ecology – up to 62 per cent of the marine iguana population on one island had been killed off.

1970 Following a military coup, Colonel Gaddafi takes over as prime minister of Libya.

17

1991 ALLIES SEND BOMBER PLANES INTO IRAQ AT THE START OF OPERATION DESERT STORM.

The Allies' aerial bombardment involved cruise missiles launched from US warships and US, British and Saudi Arabian fighter planes, bombers and helicopters aiming at military and strategic targets. The military action followed Iraq's refusal to comply with a United Nations' ultimatum for its troops to withdraw from Kuwait by 15 January. The Allies launched a land offensive on 24 February, on 25 February the Iraqis began retreating and on 27 February, US President George Bush declared victory. Kuwait was liberated but Iraqi leader Saddam Hussein remained in power in Baghdad.

On 20 March 2003, US President George W. Bush led an invasion of Iraq. Within a month, Saddam Hussein had been ousted and the Americans were claiming victory in the war. Saddam Hussein was captured after several months in hiding in December 2003. He was tried by an Iraqi court, sentenced to death and executed on 30 December 2006.

US-led coalition forces ran Iraq until power was officially handed back on 28 June 2004.

18

1997 BØRGE OUSLAND FINISHES THE FIRST UNASSISTED ANTARCTIC SOLO CROSSING.

The Norwegian polar explorer Børge Ousland, was the first person to cross the most southerly continent in the world. His expedition started on 15 November from Berkner Island in the Weddell Sea and ended when he reached the McMurdo base, by the Ross Sea, more than two months later. He had covered a distance of 2,845 km (1,768 miles), experiencing temperatures as low as −56°C (−69°F).

In 2001 Borge made the first solo crossing of the Arctic from Siberia to Canada via the North Pole in 82 days. In 2006, Borge and his expedition partner Mike Horn battled constant darkness and extreme conditions to become the first people to reach the North Pole.

19

1966 INDIRA GANDHI BECOMES INDIA'S FIRST WOMAN PRIME MINISTER.

Indira Gandhi, daughter of India's first prime minister Jawaharlal Nehru, was chosen at the end of a bitter leadership battle with former finance minister Morarji Desai. She presided over the 1971 conflict with Pakistan that created Bangladesh, and then in 1975 she was convicted of corruption and banned from holding office for six years. In response, Gandhi declared a controversial national state of emergency, which lasted for nearly two years.

Gandhi lost the 1977 general election to Morarji Desai, who headed Janata – part of an alliance of opposition parties – but returned to power in 1979. In 1984 she ordered the storming of the Golden Temple in Amritsar to flush out Sikh militants pursuing self-rule for Punjab. Two months later, her own Sikh bodyguards assassinated her. About 1,000 people, mostly Sikhs, died in the four days of rioting that followed.

Gandhi's eldest son, Rajiv, succeeded her as prime minister and was assassinated in 1991.

20

1961 DEMOCRAT JOHN F. KENNEDY BECOMES PRESIDENT OF THE USA.

John Fitzgerald Kennedy, also known as JFK, was born in Massachusetts in 1917 into a socially prominent, politically active family. At 43 years old he became the youngest person ever to be elected as president of the United States, defeating Richard Nixon. He closed his inauguration speech with the famous words:

'Ask not what your country can do for you – ask what you can do for your country.'

The Cold War between the US and the USSR, America's continuing war in Vietnam and the American Civil Rights Movement all loomed large during his short presidency. He was assassinated on 22 November 1963 in Dallas, Texas. His vice-president, Lyndon Johnson, succeeded him.

21

1950 THE AUTHOR GEORGE ORWELL DIES.

George Orwell began writing perhaps his most famous novel, *1984*, after resigning as a journalist from the BBC World Service in September 1943. It was his increasing frustration with the Ministry of Information, which censored the news during the Second World War, which led to his resignation. This subsequently became the central theme of *1984*. Words and phrases from the novel have passed into everyday usage, particularly 'Big Brother'. The book was made into a film released in 1984. George Orwell's name itself has become an adjective, 'Orwellian', meaning an oppressive system.

1984 and Orwell's satirical allegory of totalitarian rule, *Animal Farm*, frequently appear in lists of the world's best-ever selling novels.

13

22

1970 THE BOEING 747 MAKES ITS FIRST COMMERCIAL PASSENGER TRIP FROM NEW YORK TO LONDON.

The Boeing 747, commonly referred to as the 'jumbo jet', was the first long-haul, wide-body commercial airliner to cross the Atlantic. It carried 332 passengers and 18 crew on its first commercial trip, operated by PanAm Airlines from JFK International Airport to London Heathrow Airport. Nearly 40 years on, the latest version of the Boeing 747, the 747-400, flies at over 900 km/h (559 mph) and is still a popular choice for long-haul passenger flights.

23

1989 THE ARTIST SALVADOR DALÍ DIES.

Salvador Dalí was born in Catalonia, Spain in 1904. He is famous for his paintings that are considered to be part of the surrealist cultural movement. Surrealism began in the mid-1920s and the writings and artworks of surrealist artists were typified by elements of surprise and unexpected juxtapositions. In 1936, Dalí took part in the London International Surrealist Exhibition.

One of Dalí's most famous works, *The Persistence of Memory*, is sometimes referred to as *Melting Clocks*. Several of his later works incorporated holography and optical illusion, and Dalí remains an important influence on the world of art.

24

1965 FORMER BRITISH PRIME MINISTER, SIR WINSTON CHURCHILL, DIES.

Sir Winston Churchill, who died at the age of 90, was the first statesman to be given a state funeral in the twentieth century, which was held at St Paul's Cathedral in London.

Churchill served as Conservative prime minister of Britain from 1940 to 1945 and again from 1951 to 1955. He is widely regarded as a great wartime leader, and led the British war effort against the Axis powers during the Second World War. At the height of the Battle of Britain, Germany's bombing of British cities, Churchill made his famous speech praising the Allied fighter pilots with the words:

'Never in the field of human conflict was so much owed by so many to so few.'

A BBC survey in January 2000 voted Churchill the greatest British prime minister of the twentieth century, and he was voted the greatest Briton in a BBC poll in November 2002.

14 # 25

2004 THE SECOND OF TWO NASA ROVERS SENT TO EXPLORE MARS LANDS ON THE SURFACE OF THE PLANET TO LOOK FOR SIGNS OF WATER.

The *Opportunity* rover landed on the opposite side of Mars from where its sister rover, *Spirit*, had landed three weeks earlier. In March 2004 *Opportunity* showed that Mars had once had the right conditions to support life at some time in its history. Analysis of rocks at the landing site showed they had been exposed to water, and scientists now believe that the probe had landed on the shore of what had been a lake or ocean.

The two probes continued to work well and their missions were extended into late 2006. In August 2005 NASA launched a third probe, the *Mars Reconnaissance Orbiter*, to map and find water.

1971 General Idi Amin seizes power in Uganda from President Milton Obote, the man who led Uganda to independence in 1962.

26

1950 THE INDEPENDENT REPUBLIC OF INDIA IS BORN AFTER NEARLY 100 YEARS OF BRITISH RULE.

India had been running its own affairs since the actual transfer of power from British to Indian hands on 15 August 1947. Then on 26 January, India's first president, Dr

Rajendra Prasad, was sworn in, replacing the king as the country's head of state. Prasad served as prime minister for 12 years, retiring in 1962. Jawaharlal Nehru became India's first elected prime minister in the first general election in 1952. He governed the country until his death in 1964, and remains a towering figure in India's early political history.

26 January is marked with an annual public holiday in India, known as Republic Day.

27

1945 THE NOTORIOUS NAZI DEATH CAMP, AUSCHWITZ, IS LIBERATED BY THE SOVIET RED ARMY.

On 8 May 1945 a state commission compiled by the Soviets revealed the full horror of conditions in the Polish death camp. Nearly 3,000 survivors of various nationalities were questioned and the report estimated that four million people had died there between 1941 and the beginning of 1945. The dead included citizens from the Soviet Union, Poland, France, Belgium, Holland, Czechoslovakia, Yugoslavia, Hungary, Italy and Greece. The commission, which had previously investigated conditions at Majdanek, Treblinka, described Auschwitz as the worst death camp it had seen.

The final death toll at Auschwitz was later revised by the Auschwitz Museum to between one and 1.5 million, of which 800,000 were Jews.

28

1986 THE AMERICAN SPACE SHUTTLE *CHALLENGER* EXPLODES, KILLING ALL SEVEN ASTRONAUTS ON BOARD.

The five men and two women, including the first teacher in space, were just over a minute into their flight from Cape Canaveral in Florida when the *Challenger* exploded. Millions of Americans witnessed the world's worst space disaster live on television. *Challenger*'s flight, the twenty-fifth by a shuttle, had already been delayed because of bad weather.

The Rogers Commission found that the explosion had been caused by a leak through a faulty seal, or O-ring, in one of the solid rocket boosters. The *Challenger* disaster was a severe blow to the American space programme and there were no further manned flights until September 1988.

29

1996 FRANCE HALTS ITS PROGRAMME OF NUCLEAR TESTING.

The announcement by French president Jacques Chirac that France would no longer test nuclear weapons came a day after France exploded its biggest nuclear device in the South Pacific, triggering protests around the world.

A United Nations' Comprehensive Nuclear Test Ban Treaty drawn up in response to the outrage caused by the French nuclear testing programme has still not come into force. Countries including China, Israel and the United States have signed the treaty, but refused to ratify it, while India, Pakistan and North Korea have refused to sign it. In 2006 Iran provoked international concern by breaking UN seals on nuclear research facilities to resume uranium enrichment.

30

1948 AMERICAN AVIATION PIONEER ORVILLE WRIGHT DIES.
Orville Wright was born in Ohio in 1871. Along with his brother, Wilbur, he was credited with building the world's first successful aeroplane. The brothers invented 'three axis-control', which enabled a pilot to steer his aircraft effectively and maintain its position in the air. The method became standard on fixed-wing aircraft of all kinds.

Earning his place on the winning toss of a coin, Orville made the first controlled, powered human flight in their *Wright Flyer* on 17 December 1903. The flight was at an altitude of 36.5 m (120 ft) and lasted 12 seconds.

1933 Adolf Hitler becomes chancellor of Germany.

31

1983 A SEATBELT LAW IS INTRODUCED IN BRITAIN FOR DRIVERS AND FRONT-SEAT PASSENGERS.
The Department of Transport introduced the compulsory wearing of front seatbelts in cars in a bid to save lives. There had been 11 previous attempts at passing the law. In 1991 it became compulsory for adults to belt up in the back seat and in 2006, a law came in force stating that all children under the age of 12, unless they are taller than 135 cm (53 in), would have to use some form of child car seat.

February

1

1979 RELIGIOUS LEADER AYATOLLAH KHOMEINI RETURNS TO IRAN AFTER 14 YEARS IN EXILE.
Ayatollah Ruhollah Khomeini was imprisoned by the shah of Iran for his opposition to reforms in 1963. He was expelled to Iraq the following year. Khomeini spent the last few months of his exile in France, from where he coordinated the revolution in Iran in January that forced the shah to go into hiding.

Up to five million people lined the streets of the nation's capital, Tehran, to witness the homecoming of the Ayatollah – a title meaning 'Gift of God'. Armed resistance to the government mounted and Shahpur Bakhtiar stepped down as prime minister less than two weeks later, to be replaced by the Ayatollah's choice, Mehdi Bazargan.

Ayatollah Khomeini led the new regime from the theological seminary of Qum and declared an Islamic Republic in Iran at the beginning of April 1979. He died in June 1989.

2

1990 THE PRESIDENT OF SOUTH AFRICA, F. W. DE KLERK, LIFTS THE 30-YEAR BAN ON THE ANTI-APARTHEID GROUP AFRICAN NATIONAL CONGRESS (ANC).
In a televised speech at the opening of parliament, President F. W. de Klerk announced that restrictions would be lifted on the African National Congress and its ally, the South African Communist Party. This allowed active opposition to apartheid for the first time during National Party rule. He also made his first public commitment to release jailed ANC leader Nelson Mandela. Mandela was released on 11 February.

President de Klerk lifted the remaining apartheid legislation in 1991. The ANC became South Africa's first democratically elected government in April 1994, with Nelson Mandela becoming the country's first black president on 10 May 1994. Mandela retired in 1999 and was replaced as president by Thabo Mbeki.

F. W. de Klerk was awarded the joint Nobel Peace Prize with Nelson Mandela in 1993 for his role in ending apartheid in South Africa.

3

1930 THE COMMUNIST PARTY OF VIETNAM IS FOUNDED.
The Communist Party of Vietnam was founded by the Vietnamese revolutionary Ho Chi Minh and other Vietnamese exiles living in China. Ho Chi Minh became prime minister and then president of the Democratic Republic of Vietnam, and led the North Vietnamese in the Vietnam War against the US-supported Republic of Vietnam

(South Vietnam) until his death in 1969. Six years later, American forces withdrew and the war ended with a North Vietnamese victory. Vietnam was unified under the control of the Communist Party of Vietnam, which remains the only legal political party in Vietnam.

1986 Pope John Paul II meets Mother Teresa, head of the Missionaries of Charity order in Calcutta, and visits her refuge for the sick and dying.

4

1998 THOUSANDS ARE LEFT DEAD, INJURED OR HOMELESS IN AN EARTHQUAKE IN NORTHERN AFGHANISTAN.
The earthquake was centred on the city of Rostaq in the remote province of Takhar, close to the border with Tajikistan. Aftershocks continued for the next week. The first international relief workers reached the site on 7 February and Médecins Sans Frontières later confirmed that at least 4,000 had been killed and many villages were devastated. The EU offered £1.3 million of aid, including blankets, medical equipment, water and tents. The Taliban offered 100 tonnes each of rice and wheat even though the group was at war with the region.

5

1953 SWEET RATIONING ENDS IN BRITAIN.
Rationing came into force on 8 January 1940, a few months after the start of the Second World War. Many essential and non-essential foods were rationed, as well as clothing, furniture and petrol. Rationing of sweets and chocolate began on 26 July 1942. Food minister Gwilym Lloyd-George finally ended rationing when meat was taken off the ration books in July 1954.

As the first unrationed sweets went on sale, toffee apples were the biggest sellers. The de-rationing of sweets had a dramatic effect on the confectionery market. Spending on sweets and chocolate jumped by around £100 million in the first year to £250 million. Consumers in the UK now spend more than £5.5 billion on confectionery each year.

1996 The first GM (genetically modified) food – tomato puree – goes on sale in British supermarkets.

6

1952 KING GEORGE VI DIES.
As the second son of King George V, George VI was not expected to inherit the throne. He became king when his elder brother, Edward VIII, abdicated over his affair with the American divorcee Wallis Simpson, in 1936.

George VI's coronation took place on 12 May 1937. His quiet strength and courage won him the hearts of the British people when he and his wife, Queen

Elizabeth, insisted on remaining in London during the German bombing raids of the Second World War. George VI was 56 when he died at Sandringham House in Norfolk. His eldest daughter, Princess Elizabeth, succeeded him to the throne as Queen Elizabeth II. His wife became Queen Elizabeth, the Queen Mother, and she outlived him by 50 years.

7

1992 THE MAASTRICHT TREATY IS SIGNED BY MEMBERS OF THE EUROPEAN COMMUNITY.
The Maastricht Treaty, formerly known as the Treaty on European Union, was signed after final negotiations between 12 members of the European Community. It led to the creation of the European Union (EU) and signified an important step towards political and economic union between the member states. The treaty scraped through the British parliament, finally coming into force in Britain in 1993.

8

1974 US ASTRONAUTS RETURN SAFELY TO EARTH AFTER 85 DAYS IN SPACE.
Dr Edward Gibson, Lieutenant Colonel Gerald Carr and Lieutenant Colonel William Pogue spent a record-breaking 85 days in the American space station Skylab. While orbiting the Earth, the three astronauts experimented with new diets and exercise routines to counter the body changes commonly experienced by space crews. After a five-hour journey through space, the astronauts' landing craft splashed down in the Pacific Ocean.

1952 Princess Elizabeth is proclaimed Queen Elizabeth II, following the death of King George VI on 6 February.

9

1944 AMERICAN AUTHOR AND FEMINIST ALICE WALKER IS BORN.
African American Alice Walker was born in the US state of Georgia. While attending Spelman College she became involved in the US Civil Rights Movement, campaigning against the racial discrimination of African Americans. Her marriage to a Jewish civil rights lawyer became the first legal interracial marriage in their home state of Mississippi.

Walker has published novels and collections of short stories and poetry, with her work typically focusing on the struggle of African-American women against a racist and sexist society. She received the Pulitzer Prize for Fiction in 1983 for her critically acclaimed novel *The Color Purple*. She was the first African-American woman to win the prestigious award and the novel was subsequently adapted into a film in 1985 and a Broadway musical in 2005.

10

1952 THE CONGRESS PARTY OF INDIA WINS INDIA'S FIRST DEMOCRATIC ELECTIONS.

Pandit Jawaharlal Nehru led the Congress Party to victory in the country's first general election. India had gained independence from British rule in 1947, and had become a republic in 1950. Nehru had led the interim government, appointed after independence in 1947. Of the 176 million people eligible to vote in India, only 15 per cent could read or write, so symbols for each of the parties standing for election were used on ballot papers as well as their names. The Congress Party's nearest rival was the Communist Party of India (CPI).

Jawaharlal Nehru governed India until his death in 1964 and he remains an important figure in independent India's political history.

11

1990 LEADING ANTI-APARTHEID CAMPAIGNER NELSON MANDELA IS FREED FROM PRISON IN SOUTH AFRICA AFTER 27 YEARS.

Nelson Mandela's release from prison followed the relaxation of apartheid laws by South African president F. W. de Klerk. Mandela and de Klerk shared the Nobel Peace Prize in 1993 for their efforts to transform South African society and release it from the grip of apartheid.

Mandela succeeded Oliver Tambo as president of the African National Congress (ANC) in 1991. In the first multi-racial elections in the country's history in 1994, Mandela was elected president and the ANC gained 252 of the 400 seats in South Africa's national assembly. He was succeeded as ANC president by Thabo Mbeki in 1997, and stepped down in favour of Mr Mbeki as national president after the 1999 elections.

1976 John Curry wins Britain's first Olympic gold for figure-skating at the Winter Olympics in Innsbruck, Austria.

12

1994 ART THIEVES SNATCH EDVARD MUNCH'S *THE SCREAM* FROM A GALLERY IN OSLO, NORWAY.

Thieves stole one of the world's best-known paintings from the National Art Museum in the Norwegian capital Oslo, cutting *The Scream* from the wall with wire cutters. In March 1994, the museum received a £700,000 ransom demand for Edvard Munch's most renowned painting. They refused to pay, unsure that the demand was genuine. In May 1994, Norwegian and British police mounted a sting operation to retrieve the painting, and it was successfully recovered.

In January 1996, four men were convicted and sentenced in connection with the theft.

13

1959 THE FIRST BARBIE DOLL GOES ON SALE.
The fashion doll Barbie's debut was at the American Toy Fair in New York on 9 March 1959. The first Barbie doll sported a ponytail hairstyle and zebra-striped bathing suit, and was available with either blonde or brown hair. Around 350,000 dolls were sold during the first year of production. Barbie's friend, the male doll Ken arrived in 1961.

Barbie was one of the first toys to have a marketing strategy based on television advertising. It is estimated that over one billion dolls have been sold worldwide, making Barbie one of the most successful products in the history of the toy industry.

14

1945 ALLIED BOMBS DESTROY THE GERMAN CITY OF DRESDEN.
Eight hundred RAF Bomber Command planes dropped hundreds of 4,000-lb bombs in two waves of attack on the city of Dresden. With the exact number of casualties unknown, the death toll was believed to be tens of thousands. Thousands of tons of high explosive and incendiary bombs were dropped, creating a huge firestorm that destroyed the city, which was reported to be a vital command centre for the German defence against Soviet forces approaching from the east. The Allied objective had been to destroy the enemy's public morale, cut off relief supplies to the eastern front and give support to the approaching Soviet armies.

1984 Jayne Torvill and Christopher Dean's famous routine to Ravel's *Bolero* wins the ice-skating Olympic Gold for Britain at the Winter Olympics in Sarajevo, Yugoslavia.

15

1971 THE BRITISH GOVERNMENT LAUNCHES A NEW DECIMAL CURRENCY ACROSS THE COUNTRY.
The familiar pound, shilling and pence coins were phased out over the following 18 months, replaced by a decimal system dividing the pound into units of ten, including half, one, two, five, ten and 50 pence denominations. The 20 pence piece was introduced in 1982 and the half penny was withdrawn from circulation in 1984. In June 1998 the £2 coin came into general circulation.

16

1959 REVOLUTIONARY LEADER FIDEL CASTRO BECOMES CUBA'S PRIME MINISTER.
At the age of 32, Castro was sworn in as Cuba's youngest prime minister. Castro led the resistance against the seven-year military rule of President Fulgencio Batista and

commanded the 26th July Army, a guerrilla force that had driven the old regime into exile on New Year's Day. Antagonism between Cuba and the US grew, and the Americans imposed economic sanctions on Cuba from 1960. A Cuban alliance with the USSR led to the nuclear missile crisis in 1962.

In 1976, Fidel Castro passed a new constitution and became president, secretary-general of the Communist Party and commander-in-chief of the army. On 31 July 2006, Castro transferred his responsibilities to the first vice-president, his younger brother Raúl Castro.

17

1909 APACHE LEADER GERONIMO DIES.

Geronimo, born in 1829, was a prominent Native American leader of the Chiricahua Apache. He fought against the encroachment of the US on his tribal lands and people for over 25 years. A daring military leader, he led raids and war on many Mexican and later US troops, and became famous for his numerous escapes from capture between 1858 and 1886. He led the small band of Native American men, women and children that evaded 5,000 US troops for a year. He finally surrendered to the US Army General at Skeleton Canyon, Arizona on 4 September 1886.

1933 The end of the prohibition of alcohol in the United States. The consumption of alcohol had been made illegal by the introduction of the Eighteenth Amendment to the US Constitution in 1920.

18

1932 JAPAN CREATES A 'PUPPET STATE' IN THE CHINESE STATE OF MANCHURIA.

Former Qing Dynasty officials, with help from Imperial Japan, created the puppet state of Manchukuo in Manchuria, which is situated on China's eastern coast. The state was administered by Imperial Japan, with P'u Yi, the last Qing emperor, in place as a nominal regent. Manchus were actually a minority in the region, where the largest ethnic group were Han Chinese. The Qing or Manchu Dynasty ruled China from 1644 to 1911, when it was overthrown during the Xinhai Revolution.

Manchukuo's government was abolished in 1945, after the defeat of Japan in the Second World War. From 1945 to 1948, Inner Manchuria was a base for the Chinese People's Liberation Army (PLA) during the Chinese Civil War.

During the Korean War of the 1950s, the PLA crossed the Chinese-Korean border from Manchuria to recapture communist North Korea from United Nations forces.

During the 1960s the region became the site of serious tension between the Soviet Union and the People's Republic of China, resulting in the Sino-Soviet border conflict in 1969.

In 2004, Russia agreed to transfer some territory back to China, but this has yet to take place.

19

1997 CHINA'S REFORMIST LEADER DENG XIAOPING DIES.
Born in 1904, Deng Xiaoping was a prominent Chinese politician and reformer. He took power in 1978 and announced a new era of reform in China. He dismantled collective farming and allowed private enterprise, including special free-market zones, and is the man credited with opening up China economically.

Politically, Deng had a reputation as a hardliner, and repeatedly ordered crackdowns on dissidents. He was known internationally as the leader who used the army to crush the student Tiananmen Square protests in 1989, an event that caused outrage worldwide when images were seen on television.

20

1986 THE SOVIET UNION LAUNCHES THE WORLD'S BIGGEST SPACE STATION, MIR.
The Soviets' successful launch of Mir came just over three weeks after the American space shuttle *Challenger* disaster. The first crew arrived on board Mir on 15 March 1986 and it remained almost continuously occupied until November 2000. Crew member Valeri Polyakov stayed for a record 439 days.

The end of the Cold War between the United States and the Soviet Union had marked a new era of space cooperation. In September 1993 US vice-president Al Gore and Russian prime minister Viktor Chernomyrdin announced plans for a new space station, which later became the International Space Station (ISS).

Mir remained in space until 23 March 2001, during which time it orbited the Earth more than 86,000 times. It re-entered the Earth's atmosphere near Nadi, Fiji, and what was left of the 135-tonne craft fell into the South Pacific Ocean.

21

1965 BLACK NATIONALIST LEADER MALCOLM X IS ASSASSINATED.
Controversial black leader Malcolm X, who had once called for a 'blacks-only' state in the United States, was shot as he began a speech just outside Harlem in New York. Malcolm X gave up his 'slave' family name of Little when he joined the black Muslim group Nation of Islam. But he broke away from the group acrimoniously in 1963 to set up his own organisation for:

'Negro intellectuals who favoured racial separation but could not accept the Muslim religion.'

In March 1966 three men, two of whom admitted being members of the Nation of Islam, were found guilty of Malcolm X's murder. They were sentenced to life imprisonment.

22

1997 SCIENTISTS IN SCOTLAND ANNOUNCE THE BIRTH OF THE WORLD'S FIRST SUCCESSFULLY CLONED MAMMAL, DOLLY THE SHEEP.
Dolly, who was created at the Roslin Institute in Edinburgh, was the first mammal to have been successfully cloned from an adult cell. Previous clonings had been from embryo cells. Scientists cloned Dolly by inserting DNA from a single sheep cell into an egg and implanting it in a surrogate mother. DNA tests revealed that Dolly is identical to the ewe that donated the udder cell and is unrelated to the surrogate mother.

The sheep's birth was heralded as one of the most significant scientific breakthroughs of the decade, enabling scientists to study genetic diseases for which there are currently no cure. But it also sparked ethical controversy and raised moral dilemmas amid fears that the technique could be used to clone humans.

The decision was made in 2003 to put down Dolly, after a veterinary examination showed she had a progressive lung disease. Her preserved body went on display at the National Museum of Scotland in Edinburgh.

23

1919 BENITO MUSSOLINI FORMS THE FASCIST PARTY IN ITALY.
Benito Mussolini was the prime minister of Italy from 1922 until he was overthrown in 1943. In 1919, he had formed the Italian Fighting League, with just 200 members. It soon became an organised political movement, the Fascisti, with a brutal army of so-called Blackshirts terrorising anarchists, socialists and communists. Appointed prime minister by the king, Mussolini established a fascist dictatorship that valued nationalism and military power.

He was a close ally of German dictator Adolf Hitler, and in June 1940 he entered the Second World War on the side of Nazi Germany. The Allies defeated Italy in 1943, by which time Mussolini had been replaced by Marshal Pietro Badoglio. Mussolini was shot by Italian Partisans on 27 April 1945.

24

1981 PRINCE CHARLES AND LADY DIANA SPENCER ANNOUNCE THEIR ENGAGEMENT.
The Prince of Wales and Lady Diana Spencer went on to marry on 29 July 1981 at St Paul's Cathedral in London, watched on live television by an estimated 750 million people around the world. Their first child, Prince William, was born on 21 June 1982 and their second, Prince Harry, on 15 September 1984, when it became clear the marriage was in difficulty. The couple separated in 1993 and officially divorced in 1996.

Diana, Princess of Wales, died in a car accident in Paris on 31 August 1997 and Prince Charles married his long-standing girlfriend Camilla Parker Bowles on 9 April 2005.

25

1964 CASSIUS CLAY BECOMES WORLD HEAVYWEIGHT BOXING CHAMPION.
The 22-year-old Cassius Clay beat Sonny Liston in one of the biggest upsets in boxing history. Shortly after the fight, Clay surprised the sports world by announcing that he had joined the Nation of Islam and had changed his name to Muhammad Ali. His boxing career lasted 20 years, during which he won 56 fights and scored 37 knock-outs. As an admirer once said, Ali would 'float like a butterfly, sting like a bee'. Muhammad Ali said the early victory over Liston was the most important of his career.

In December 1981, Ali decided to retire from the ring. He was later diagnosed with Parkinson's disease.

26

1987 THE CHURCH OF ENGLAND VOTES FOR THE ORDINATION OF WOMEN PRIESTS.
The Church of England had been debating the issue of women priests for ten years and the final go-ahead was given by the general synod in 1992. The first woman priest was ordained in Bristol on 12 March 1994. By April 1998 there were more than 1,700 women priests.

The Church of England set up a working party in 2000 to consider the licensing of women bishops. The general synod voted on the issue in summer 2005 and put the wheels in motion for the ordination of women bishops.

27

1964 THE ITALIAN GOVERNMENT APPEALS FOR HELP TO SAVE THE LEANING TOWER OF PISA.
The Tower of Pisa is the freestanding bell tower of the cathedral in Pisa. Although intended to stand vertically, the tower began leaning to the south-east soon after it was constructed in 1173, due to poorly laid foundations. In 1964, the Italian government requested aid in preventing the tower from toppling. A multinational group of engineers and mathematicians discussed stabilisation methods. The tower was eventually closed to the public in January 1990.

After a decade of corrective reconstruction and stabilisation efforts, soil was removed from underneath the raised end and the tower was straightened by 45 centimeters. The tower was reopened to the public on 15 December 2001.

28

1991 GULF WAR CEASEFIRE.
President George Bush announced the ceasefire after Iraq accepted all 12 resolutions made by the United Nations. Iraq had refused to comply with the UN ultimatum for

its troops to withdraw from Kuwait after its invasion in August 1990. On 16 January 1991, Operation Desert Storm began with the Allies launching an aerial bombardment involving cruise missiles launched from US warships and US, British and Saudi Arabian fighter planes and bombers. A land offensive was launched on 24 February.

Kuwait was liberated but Saddam Hussein remained in power. Tensions between Iraq and the US continued and in March 2003 US President George W. Bush launched an attack on Iraq, in spite of worldwide opposition to war. Backed by British and Australian forces, the aim was to topple Saddam Hussein and eliminate any weapons of mass destruction. Saddam Hussein was captured alive after several months in hiding in December 2003. Following a trial in an Iraqi court he was sentenced to death and executed in December 2006.

American-led coalition forces continue to occupy Iraq. On 28 June 2004, power was officially handed back to the Iraqi authorities and elections were held in February 2005.

29

1996 THE SIEGE OF THE BOSNIAN CAPITAL OF SARAJEVO IS LIFTED.
The siege of Sarajevo ended after almost four years of continuous shelling and sniper attacks. The Muslim-led Bosnian government took back control after the longest siege in the history of modern warfare. Under the terms of the Dayton peace agreement, signed in December 1995, the Bosnian Serbs were to give up control of five suburbs and return them to Muslim-Croat authority. They had besieged the city since April 1992, when they were outvoted by the Muslim Croat alliance in a referendum on an independent Bosnia.

General Stanislav Galic, who commanded the Bosnian Serb forces that besieged the Bosnian capital during the war, was found guilty by the war crimes tribunal. Bosnian Serb president Radovan Karadzic and General Ratko Mladic, his army chief, were both indicted for war crimes but continue to evade arrest.

March

1

1954 THE UNITED STATES TESTS THE HYDROGEN BIKINI BOMB.

The Bikini bomb was the biggest man-made explosion until the USSR's 50-megaton test in 1961. The 15-megaton hydrogen bomb went off in the Pacific archipelago of Bikini, part of the Marshall Islands. It was believed to be up to 1,000 times more powerful than the atomic bomb that destroyed Hiroshima at the end of the Second World War. More than 250 people were accidentally exposed to radiation because the explosion and fall-out were far greater than expected.

The original natives of Bikini eventually returned to their homes in 1974. They were evacuated four years later when new tests showed there were still high levels of residual radioactivity in the region. Twenty-three nuclear tests were carried out at Bikini between 1946 and 1958.

2

1969 CONCORDE, THE WORLD'S FIRST SUPERSONIC AIRLINER, MAKES ITS MAIDEN FLIGHT.

The Anglo-French supersonic airliner Concorde took off from Toulouse and was in the air for just 27 minutes before the pilot, Andre Turcat, made the decision to land. The test flight reached 3,000 m (9,840 ft), but Concorde's speed never rose above 480 km/h (300 mph). Concorde completed its first actual supersonic flight on 1 October 1969 and the first commercial flights took place on 21 January 1976 when British Airways flew from London Heathrow to Bahrain and Air France from Paris to Rio.

Concorde's heavy fuel consumption and small tanks made it incredibly uneconomic to fly, and in April 2003, British Airways and Air France announced that the plane would be retired. Concorde's final commercial flight was on 23 October 2003.

1970 The prime minister of Rhodesia, Ian Smith declares Rhodesia to be a republic, cutting its last line with the British Crown.

3

1985 MINERS' LEADERS VOTE TO END THE LONGEST-RUNNING INDUSTRIAL DISPUTE IN BRITISH HISTORY.

On 6 March 1984 the British government had announced plans to cut coal production by the equivalent of 20 pits, or 20,000 jobs. The flashpoint for strike action was in South Yorkshire, where miners were told that the Cortonwood Pit would close even though there was still workable coal. Miners walked out and were soon joined by colleagues around the country. After one year's strike action, miners' leaders voted to call off their strike against Conservative prime minister Margaret Thatcher's government. There was no peace deal over pit closures, but miners' leader Arthur Scargill said the campaign against job losses would continue.

4

1980 NATIONALIST LEADER ROBERT MUGABE BECOMES ZIMBABWE'S FIRST BLACK PRIME MINISTER.

Mugabe's radical Zimbabwe African National Union (Patriotic Front) party or Zanu (PF) won 57 of the 80 black seats being contested in the country's first election since the end of white minority rule.

Mugabe arrived in the country only six weeks before the election, after spending 10 years in exile. He had fought a lengthy guerrilla war against the white minority government in the capital, Salisbury, at first as part of Joshua Nkomo's Zimbabwe African People's Union and later as leader of the breakaway Zanu (PF) Party.

In March 2002, Mugabe was elected for a controversial fifth term as president amid much speculation about ballot-rigging. As his political fortunes have declined he has resurrected land redistribution as an issue and many white farmers have been forced to leave the land they had farmed for generations. The Zimbabwe economy currently has inflation running at 120 per cent and hundreds of thousands of people are dependent on food aid.

1975 Silent film legend Charlie Chaplin receives a knighthood at the age of 85.

5

1936 FIRST FLIGHT OF THE SUPERMARINE SPITFIRE PLANE.

The Supermarine Spitfire was a British single-seat fighter plane used by the Royal Air Force (RAF) and its Allies during the Second World War. The Spitfire was designed by R. J. Mitchell and had an elliptical wing with a thin cross-section, which allowed a higher top speed than other contemporary designs. The planes were produced from 1938 to 1948.

Spitfires played a crucial part in Britain's victory against the German invaders during the Battle of Britain. The main adversary of the Spitfire was its German counterpart, the Messerschmitt BF 109.

6

1957 GHANA BECOMES THE FIRST BLACK AFRICAN COUNTRY TO GAIN INDEPENDENCE.

Tens of thousands of Ghanaians gathered in the capital, Accra, to greet the independent country's first prime minister, Dr Kwame Nkrumah. As part of the celebrations marking the end of colonial rule, the Independence Monument was erected near the spot where in 1948, members of the Ghanaian ex-servicemen's union were shot when marching to present a petition to the British governor.

28

In 1960, Prime Minister Nkrumah declared Ghana a republic, and himself president for life in 1964, banning all opposition parties. He was deposed in 1966 by a military coup and later died in exile in Romania in 1972.

7

1969 GOLDA MEIR IS ACCEPTED AS THE SUCCESSOR TO THE PRIME MINISTER OF ISRAEL.

Following her appointment, the 'grand old woman of Israeli politics' won a convincing vote of confidence when she presented an identical cabinet to parliament to that of her predecessor. She went on to win Israel's general election in October 1969. The Israeli prime minister governed using coalitions. For the next four years she remained in control but she was blamed for being caught off guard when war broke out between Israeli and Arab forces in 1973. The Arabs were eventually defeated by a sustained Israeli counter-attack but Meir's reputation never recovered. She won the general election in 1973 but resigned in April 1974. She died in 1978.

8

1918 THE FIRST RECORDED CASE OF SPANISH FLU OCCURS AT THE START OF A WORLDWIDE FLU PANDEMIC.

The flu pandemic, commonly referred to as Spanish Flu, lasted from 1918 to 1919 and was caused by an unusually severe and deadly influenza virus. Current estimates say that up to 100 million people were killed worldwide, in a global pandemic spreading even to the Arctic and remote Pacific islands. The high death toll was caused by the extremely high infection rate and the severity of the symptoms. The majority of deaths were from the secondary infection, bacterial pneumonia. The pandemic was unusual because it mostly killed young adults, whereas influenza is normally most deadly to the very young and the very old.

2001 The wreck of Donald Campbell's speedboat, *Bluebird*, is recovered from the bottom of Coniston Water in Cumbria. The boat had lain there since the accident in 1967 that killed Campbell as he attempted to break the world water speed record.

9

1973 THE PEOPLE OF NORTHERN IRELAND VOTE TO REMAIN WITHIN THE UNITED KINGDOM.

In a referendum on the future of the province, 57 per cent of the electorate voted to retain links with the UK. The turn-out was reported to be 59 per cent of the electorate, although less then one per cent of Catholics voted. The Unionist victory came following a series of bomb attacks in London. The vote was followed by a white paper on Northern Ireland, published on 20 March 1973. The new Northern Ireland assembly met for the first time on 31 July 1973.

London's direct rule over Northern Ireland stayed in place for 26 years.

10

2006 NASA'S *MARS RECONNAISSANCE ORBITER* ARRIVES AT MARS.
The *Mars Reconnaissance Orbiter* (MRO) is a multipurpose spacecraft designed to conduct reconnaissance and exploration of Mars from orbit. It was launched on 12 August 2005 and attained Martian orbit on 10 March 2006. MRO contains equipment to analyse the landforms, minerals and ice of Mars in an attempt to accurately map the Martian landscape. Its telecommunications system transfers more data back to Earth than all previous interplanetary missions combined.

11

1985 MIKHAIL GORBACHEV BECOMES SOVIET LEADER.
Following the death of Konstantin Chernenko, Mikhail Gorbachev took over as general secretary of the Soviet Communist Party. Gorbachev radically changed the course of Soviet foreign policy, signing a number of agreements with the United States on nuclear disarmament. He introduced a policy of openness, or 'glasnost', and was also the architect of 'perestroika', or deep political and economic reforms. Growing nationalist movements led by the Baltic States led him to propose a loose federation of Soviet states, but this was unacceptable to communist hardliners. In August 1991 he survived a coup attempt – largely thanks to the support of the Russian authorities, under the leadership of Boris Yeltsin.

Gorbachev resigned on 25 December 1991 and the Soviet flag, the hammer and sickle, was lowered for the last time on 31 December. Gorbachev is now president of the Green Cross, an organisation concerned with the clean-up of chemical and biological weapons.

1955 Sir Alexander Fleming, the man who first discovered the life-saving drug penicillin, dies.

12

1999 VIOLINIST YEHUDI MENUHIN DIES.
The career of one of the twentieth century's finest musicians spanned more than seven decades. Born on 22 April 1916 in New York of Russian Jewish parents, Menuhin made his debut in San Francisco as a child prodigy and by the age of 13 had performed in London, Paris and Berlin. As well as performing classical works, Menuhin played duets with the renowned jazz violinist Stephane Grappelli, as well as the sitar star Ravi Shankar.

Menuhin also became a campaigner for human rights. He went to Germany after the Second World War to play for the survivors of the Belsen concentration camp. He was knighted in 1987 and became a life peer in 1993. Following his death, world leaders – including the secretary-general of the United Nations, Kofi Annan, made tributes. Annan praised Menuhin as a musician and campaigner for world peace and human rights.

13

1996 GUN MASSACRE AT A SCHOOL IN DUNBLANE, SCOTLAND.
Thomas Hamilton marched into a school in Dunblane and killed 17 children and their teacher, before turning the gun on himself. A public inquiry into the massacre found Hamilton had licences for six guns. A massive campaign was launched after the tragedy for tighter gun controls. The Snowdrop Campaign was successful in achieving a change in the law in 1997, making it illegal to buy or possess a handgun.

14

1960 RADIO TELESCOPE MAKES SPACE HISTORY.
The British radio telescope at Jodrell Bank in Cheshire set a new space record by making contact with the American *Pioneer V* satellite at a distance of 8,000 km (4,970 miles) from Earth. The previous record had been set by the Soviet satellite *Lunik III*, which photographed the far side of the Moon in 1959. Jodrell Bank was the world's largest fully steerable radio telescope.

The American satellite was launched from Cape Canaveral in Florida three days earlier, on 11 March. Jodrell Bank first made contact with *Pioneer V* after it went into orbit around the Sun, between the paths of Earth and Venus. In April 1960, the command centre in Hawaii began having problems contacting *Pioneer V* and Jodrell Bank began to play a bigger role in controlling the satellite.

31

15

1917 RUSSIAN TSAR NICHOLAS II ABDICATES.
Nicholas II was the last emperor of Russia. He ruled from 1894 until his forced abdication by communist revolutionaries in 1917. The outbreak of the First World War in 1914 had put Russia under attack from the combined forces of the German and Austro-Hungarian empires. As commander-in-chief, Nicholas II was directly linked to the losses suffered by the Russian Army and the hardships of his people.

Political unrest swept through the country. Led by revolutionary Vladimir Lenin, the Bolsheviks were a faction of the Marxist Russian Social Democratic Labour Party. Having deposed Nicholas II and shot him and his family, they went on to seize power in Russia during the Russian Revolution of 1917, and founded the Soviet Union.

16

1953 MARSHAL TITO OF YUGOSLAVIA BECOMES THE FIRST COMMUNIST HEAD OF STATE TO VISIT BRITAIN.
Marshal Josef Tito of Yugoslavia was invited to Britain following the death of Soviet leader Joseph Stalin, who had expelled Yugoslavia from the Cominform group of communist nations in 1948 for failing to adhere to Soviet policies. Since that time Yugoslavia had relied on western aid for food and armaments.

Tito had formed Communist Yugoslavia in 1945. He maintained Yugoslavia's independence from the USSR and developed his own form of Communism with power decentralised to workers' councils. He dealt with nationalist aspirations by creating a federation of six republics: Croatia, Montenegro, Serbia, Slovenia, Bosnia-Herzegovina and Macedonia. In 1980, the federation fell apart rapidly after Slovenia's declaration of independence.

17

1942 US GENERAL DOUGLAS MACARTHUR ARRIVES IN AUSTRALIA TO BECOME SUPREME ALLIED COMMANDER IN THE PACIFIC DURING THE SECOND WORLD WAR.

Born in Arkansas in 1880, general of the US Army Douglas MacArthur played a prominent role in the Pacific conflict between the US and Japan during the Second World War. He commanded the invasion of Japan, officially accepting their surrender on 2 September 1945 and overseeing the US occupation of Japan from 1945 to 1951. MacArthur led the United Nations Command forces defence of South Korea between 1950 and 1951 against North Korea's communist invasion.

In 1942 MacArthur was awarded the Medal of Honor, the highest military decoration given in the United States.

1969 Golda Meir officially becomes the first female prime minister of Israel.

18

1915 FAILED ALLIED NAVAL ATTACK IN THE BATTLE OF GALLIPOLI.

The Battle of Gallipoli took place from April 1915 to December 1915 during the First World War. A joint British and French operation was mounted to capture the Turkish capital of Istanbul. The German Empire and her allies Austria-Hungary blocked Russia's land trade routes to Europe and the Allied forces needed to provide a secure sea route for military and trade.

On 18 March, the Allied attack targeted the narrowest point of the Dardanelles. But Turkish sea mines damaged all 16 battleships and three ships were sunk. This naval defeat led to an attempt to use ground forces, but this also failed, with heavy casualties on both sides.

In Turkey, the Battle of Gallipoli is seen as a defining moment in the country's history. It laid the grounds for the Turkish War of Independence, which led to the foundation of the Turkish Republic.

19

1982 ARGENTINE FLAG IS HOISTED AT THE BRITISH COLONY OF THE FALKLAND ISLANDS IN THE SOUTH ATLANTIC.

The action was seen as a highly provocative move in the ongoing dispute between Britain and Argentina over the sovereignty of the islands, which had been claimed by

Britain in 1833. On 2 April Argentine forces invaded the islands after deciding to use force instead of diplomacy to regain the territories. Many did not expect Britain to retaliate but on 5 April the British government sent a task force to the Falklands. In the ensuing war, 655 Argentines and 255 British died. The conflict ended on 14 June when the commander of the Argentine garrison at Port Stanley surrendered to British troops.

20

1966 FOOTBALL'S WORLD CUP IS STOLEN.
The World Cup was stolen while it was on exhibition at Central Hall in Westminster, London. Thieves removed the solid gold Jules Rimet trophy from the 'Sport with Stamps' display at the Stampex exhibition, but left behind stamps worth £3 million.

On 27 March, Pickles, a mongrel dog, found the trophy in south London while out for a walk with his owner. Later that year it was England who won the World Cup, but in 1970 Brazil was allowed to keep the trophy forever, after winning the competition for the third time. The replacement trophy remains the current prize for the World Cup.

21

1918 THE START OF THE SECOND BATTLE OF THE SOMME DURING THE FIRST WORLD WAR.
33

The two Battles of the Somme were fought on the Western Front, the armed frontier between lands controlled by Germany to the east and the Allies Britain and France to the west in the basin of the Somme River in France. The second battle followed the abandoned first Battle of the Somme in 1916, when the Allied offensive against German troops was launched on 1 July and ran until 18 November. During the months of trench warfare, the Allies had gained just 12 km (7.5 miles) of ground, at a cost of an estimated 420,000 British and 200,000 French casualties.

The Second Battle of the Somme marked the last great series of German offensives during the First World War. The immediate German objective was to capture Amiens before proceeding to the French capital, Paris. A major Allied counter-offensive from July to November 1918 drove the German forces back to produce a German defeat and the end of the First World War.

22

1945 THE ARAB LEAGUE IS FORMED.
The Arab League, also called the League of the Arab States, is a regional organisation of Arab States in the Middle East and North Africa. It was formed with six members: Egypt, Iraq, Transjordan (renamed Jordan in 1950), Lebanon, Saudi Arabia and Syria. Yemen joined later that same year, and the number of member states has continued to grow to the current 22.

The league is involved in political, economic and cultural programmes to promote the interests of the member states.

23

1933 THE ENABLING ACT IS PASSED BY THE GERMAN REICHSTAG.

The Enabling Act's formal name was the 'Law to Remedy the Distress of the People and the Nation'. It was passed by Germany's parliament, the Reichstag, and allowed Adolf Hitler, chancellor and leader of National Socialist German Workers' Party, or Nazi Party, to enact laws without the involvement of the German government.

Under Hitler, the Nazis gained power and influence after Germany's defeat at the end of the First World War in 1918. They used propaganda and violence to establish a nationalist, anti-Jewish and anti-communist regime, while rearming the military and pursuing an aggressive foreign policy. Hitler became führer in 1934 and his totalitarian dictatorship was responsible for the start of the Second World War in 1939.

1919 Benito Mussolini founds the Fascist Party in Italy.

24

1944 ALLIED PRISONERS BREAK OUT OF THE GERMAN PRISONER-OF-WAR CAMP STALAG LUFT III.

Stalag Luft III in Poland housed captured Allied airmen. Its site was selected because it would be difficult to escape from, but the camp is best known for two famous prisoner escapes via tunnelling that took place there.

The Stalag Luft III compound eventually grew to house 10,000 prisoners. The barracks were raised off the ground to make it easier for guards to detect any tunnelling activity and microphones were placed around the perimeter of the camp as a further deterrent. However, in January 1943, Roger Bushell led a plot for a major escape from the camp. The plan was to dig three deep tunnels, codenamed 'Tom', 'Dick' and 'Harry'. The depth of the tunnels, about 9 m (30 ft) meant that they were below the detection level of the microphones and prisoners installed small railcar systems in them for moving sand.

Out of 76 escapees, 73 were captured. The prisoners' heroic attempts were captured in the popular 1963 film *The Great Escape*.

25

1980 THE BRITISH OLYMPIC ASSOCIATION VOTES TO ATTEND THE OLYMPIC GAMES IN MOSCOW.

The British government had placed pressure on the British Olympic Association (BOA) not to attend the Games after the Soviet Union's invasion of Afghanistan in December 1979.

Many countries did join the US-led boycott against the twenty-second Olympics, which were the first Games ever held in Europe. The International Olympics Committee condemned the boycott and said athletics should not be concerned with politics. At the time, South Africa was banned from participating because of its policy of discriminating against blacks.

British athlete Steve Ovett won the 800 metres gold, beating the world record holder, fellow Brit Sebastian Coe, who won the silver medal. Coe won the 1,500 metres gold for Britain, with Ovett winning the bronze medal.

26

1979 HISTORIC ISRAEL AND EGYPT PEACE DEAL.

Israel and Egypt ended 30 years of war with an historic peace treaty brokered by the United States. The ceremony on the White House lawn in Washington, D.C. was broadcast live on television. President Anwar al-Sadat of Egypt, and the Israeli prime minister Menachem Begin described the ceremony as an 'historic turning point'.

The Egypt-Israel peace treaty was a direct result of the Camp David Peace Accords, signed in September 1978. Under the accords, Israel agreed to withdraw troops from the Sinai Peninsula in return for Egypt's recognition of the state of Israel. Palestinians were also granted the right to some self-determination. The last Israeli troops left the Sinai Peninsula in 1982. Less than two months later Israel invaded Lebanon. There was little further progress towards peace in the Middle East until the Oslo Peace Process began in 1993.

President Sadat and Prime Minister Begin were jointly awarded the Nobel Peace Prize later that year.

27

35

1958 NIKITA KHRUSHCHEV BECOMES PREMIER OF THE SOVIET UNION.

Khrushchev was born into a Russian peasant family in 1894. He succeeded Joseph Stalin as first secretary of the Communist Party of the Soviet Union from 1953 to 1964, and was Soviet premier from 1958 to 1964.

He pursued a course of reform and denounced the 'cult of personality' surrounding Stalin, who he accused of crimes committed during the campaigns of political repression known as the Great Purges, during the 1930s. In 1958 he replaced Nicolai Bulganin as prime minister and established himself as the leader of both state and party, becoming premier on 27 March. Under Khrushchev the Soviet Union pursued an impressive space exploration programme and political tensions increased between the Soviet Union and the United States in what became known as the Cold War.

28

1939 GENERAL FRANCO CONQUERS THE SPANISH CAPITAL MADRID DURING THE SPANISH CIVIL WAR.

The Spanish Civil War started on 17 July 1936 after an attempted coup by parts of the army against the government of the Second Spanish Republic. The conflict lasted until 1 April 1939, when the nationalist rebels founded a dictatorship led by General Francisco Franco. The supporters of the Republic gained the support of the Soviet Union while the nationalist rebels received the support of Italy and Germany in a conflict from which the Spanish people and economy took decades to recover.

29

1981 THE FIRST LONDON MARATHON TAKES PLACE.

Around 6,700 people competed in the first-ever London marathon, following a route from Greenwich Park, in south-east London, to Buckingham Palace. A mark of the success of the first London Marathon could be seen the following year when more than 90,000 people from across the world applied to take part in the run.

It is now an annual charity fundraising event, with the number of participants averaging more than 30,000. The marathon's founder, Chris Brasher, died in February 2003.

30

1981 US PRESIDENT RONALD REAGAN IS SHOT.

President Ronald Reagan was shot and wounded after a lone gunman opened fire in Washington, D.C. The Republican president had only been in office for 69 days. Reagan was operated on and made a fast recovery. John Hinckley was charged with trying to assassinate the president and the following June he was found not guilty by reason of insanity and committed to hospital.

Ronald Reagan went on to win a second term in office in 1984. He died in June 2004.

2002 Queen Elizabeth, the Queen Mother dies.

31

1959 THE DALAI LAMA ESCAPES TO INDIA.

The spiritual leader of Tibet, the Dalai Lama, crossed the border into India after an epic 15-day journey on foot over the Himalayan mountains. Many thought he had been killed in the fierce Chinese crackdown that had followed the Tibetan uprising earlier in the month. The Dalai Lama was offered asylum in India and settled in Dharamsala, in northern India. He was followed into exile by about 80,000 Tibetans, most of whom settled in the same area, which became known as 'Little Lhasa'. Tibet is still under Chinese control.

The Dalai Lama was awarded the Nobel Peace Prize in 1989, and has become a symbol of peaceful resistance to oppression throughout the world.

April

1

1999 LABOUR INTRODUCES A MINIMUM RATE OF PAY IN BRITAIN FOR THE FIRST TIME.
The Labour legislation stated that all adults must be paid at least £3.60 an hour and workers under the age of 22 must get no less than £3 an hour. Firms faced a fine of up to £5,000 for each worker who was paid below the statutory minimum. The change was expected to benefit about two million people, more than half of whom worked in the service sector. In 2002 the minimum wage reached £4.10 an hour for adults and £3.50 for those under 22. Trade unions have consistently pushed for a rate of at least £5 per hour for all workers.

2001 Former Yugoslav president Slobodan Milosevic is arrested for war crimes committed during the conflicts in Bosnia, Croatia and Kosovo.

2

2005 POPE JOHN PAUL II DIES.
Pope John Paul II, head of the Catholic Church, died in his private apartment at the Vatican, aged 84. Many thousands of people gathered in Rome's St Peter's Square to pay tribute to the pope, who was buried on 8 April in St Peter's Basilica, after a funeral in Rome.

   Polish-born Karol Wojtyla became pope in 1978. He was the first elected non-Italian pope for 450 years and the third longest-serving pontiff in history. Pope John Paul II visited more than 120 countries during his 26-year papacy. He took a conservative stand on issues like abortion and contraception, and was a tireless advocate of peace around the world. He was succeeded by Pope Benedict XVI, who was elected pope on 19 April.

1982 Argentina invades the British territory of the Falkland Islands in the south Atlantic Ocean.

3

1922 JOSEPH STALIN BECOMES THE FIRST GENERAL SECRETARY OF THE COMMUNIST PARTY OF THE SOVIET UNION.
Joseph Stalin remained general secretary of the Communist Party of the Soviet Union until his death in 1953. His increasing control of the party from 1928 onwards led to him becoming party leader and dictator of the country.

Under Stalin's leadership the Soviet Union joined with Britain and France to defeat Hitler's Nazi Germany during the Second World War. The Soviet Union became a world superpower, but Stalin's politically repressive regime and programmes of industrialisation and collectivisation during the 1930s cost millions of people their lives.

4

1968 AMERICAN BLACK CIVIL RIGHTS LEADER MARTIN LUTHER KING JR IS ASSASSINATED.

Martin Luther King Jr was shot dead in the US city of Memphis, where he was to lead a march of sanitation workers protesting against low wages and poor working conditions. The charismatic civil rights leader joined the crusade for equal rights for black people in America in the mid-1950s and was one of the leaders of the Alabama bus boycott in 1955. In 1963 King led a massive march on Washington, D.C. where he delivered his famous 'I have a dream' speech. He advocated the use of non-violent action and in 1964 was awarded the Nobel Peace Prize. Martin Luther King Jr's assassination led to riots in more than 100 US cities.

James Earl Ray confessed to and was convicted of King's murder and sentenced to 99 years in prison. He later retracted his confession, dying in prison in 1998.

5

1976 JAMES CALLAGHAN BECOMES THE NEW LABOUR PRIME MINISTER OF BRITAIN.

James Callaghan became prime minister following the surprise resignation of long-standing Labour leader and prime minister Harold Wilson the month before. He beat his main rival, employment secretary Michael Foot, by 176 votes to 137 to become Britain's new prime minister.

Shortly after Callaghan came to power, his Labour government lost its slim majority and was forced to make a series of deals with minority parties to survive, including the alliance with the Liberal Party in 1977, known as the Lib-Lab Pact. Following the 'winter of discontent' in 1978, with its power cuts and strikes, the Labour government lost a no-confidence motion in March 1979 and was forced to call a general election. The Conservatives won under Margaret Thatcher, and Labour remained out of office for the next 18 years.

1976 Reclusive American billionaire Howard Hughes dies aged 70.

6

1930 THE END OF GANDHI'S SALT MARCH TO DANDI IN INDIA.

The Salt March to Dandi, also known as the Salt Satyagraha, was an act of non-violent protest against the British salt tax in colonial India. The tax was one of many economic means used to generate revenue to support British colonial rule.

Mahatma Gandhi walked from Sabarmati Ashram to Dandi, Gujarat to make salt. He was a major political and spiritual leader of India and the Indian independence movement. He resisted tyranny through mass, non-violent civil disobedience and inspired movements for civil rights and freedom across the world. Large numbers of Indians followed him on his salt march of their own accord and the protest lasted from 12 March to 6 April 1930.

Indian independence was not achieved until 1947, with India declaring itself a republic in 1950. Gandhi is officially honoured as the Father of the Nation in India.

7

1948 THE WORLD HEALTH ORGANISATION IS ESTABLISHED.
The World Health Organisation (WHO) is an agency of the United Nations (UN) that coordinates international public health issues. Its headquarters are situated in Geneva, Switzerland.

WHO coordinates international efforts to monitor outbreaks of infectious diseases such as AIDS and malaria. It supports the development and distribution of safe vaccines and drugs, and carries out campaigns, for example to discourage tobacco consumption. The organisation endorsed the world's first official HIV/AIDS Toolkit for Zimbabwe from October 2006, making it an international standard.

1917 The United States declares war on Germany during the First World War.

39

8

1973 SPANISH ARTIST PABLO PICASSO DIES.
Born in Spain in 1881, Pablo Picasso exhibited his first paintings in Barcelona at the age of 12. During his lifetime he is said to have produced around 20,000 paintings, sculptures and drawings. Picasso was an avid art collector, and left a personal art collection including works by Paul Cézanne, Georges Braque and Henri Matisse to the Louvre Museum in Paris.

Picasso was a lifelong communist, who supported the republican government defeated by General Franco's forces during the Spanish Civil War. One of his best-known paintings is *Guernica*, inspired by the destruction of a small Basque town during the war. *Guernica* is on display at Madrid's Museo Nacional Centro de Arte Reina Sofía. In 1980 more than one million people visited the Museum of Modern Art in New York to view an exhibition of Picasso's work.

9

2005 PRINCE CHARLES MARRIES CAMILLA PARKER BOWLES.
The Prince of Wales and Camilla Parker Bowles married during a private civil wedding at Windsor's Guildhall, more than 30 years after their romance first began. The couple had both been married before and Diana, Princess of Wales had claimed that there were 'three people' in her marriage.

After the wedding ceremony Charles and Camilla returned to Windsor Castle for a service of blessing led by the archbishop of Canterbury. Camilla Parker Bowles became the Duchess of Cornwall on her marriage to the heir to the throne.

Prince Charles married Lady Diana Spencer in 1981, and had two sons, Princes William and Harry. Charles and Diana divorced in 1996, with Diana famously referring to Camilla as one of the contributing factors in the breakdown of their marriage. Camilla Parker Bowles had been married previously to cavalry officer Andrew Parker Bowles, with whom she has two children. Controversy remains as to whether Camilla, as a divorcee, can ever become queen of England.

10

1998 NORTHERN IRELAND PEACE TALKS END WITH THE HISTORIC GOOD FRIDAY AGREEMENT.

The Good Friday Agreement was reached after nearly two years of talks and 30 years of conflict in Northern Ireland between republicans and unionists. It was seen as a triumph for British prime minister Tony Blair and the Republic of Ireland's leader, Bertie Ahern, who had succeeded in securing peace where their predecessors had failed.

A referendum held in May 1998 on both sides of the Irish border returned a resounding 'yes' vote for the peace agreement and David Trimble became the first elected prime minister.

Disagreement over the disposal of illegal weapons by paramilitary groups and policing led to three suspensions of the Northern Ireland Assembly and in October 2002 it was also suspended after allegations of IRA (Irish Republican Army) intelligence gathering inside the Northern Ireland Office. Devolved power was restored to the Assembly on 8 May 2007. Age-old opponents, Democratic Unionist Party leader Ian Paisley and Sinn Fein's Martin McGuinness, took office as first minister and deputy first minister.

11

1981 THE START OF THREE-DAY RACE RIOTS IN BRIXTON, SOUTH LONDON.

The arrest of a black man led to hundreds of youths taking to the streets of Brixton in south London. They hurled petrol bombs at police, burnt cars and looted shops. A charge by 200 officers with riot shields and batons failed when they were forced to retreat under a hail of missiles. Nearly 300 police officers and 65 civilians were injured during three days of rioting in Brixton.

Many local people blamed the police's Operation Swamp for triggering the riots. Young black men felt they were being singled out and questioned under the controversial 'Sus' law. Following the riots there was an inquiry and major changes were implemented in policing, including an end to 'Sus' and the setting up of the Police Complaints Authority.

1957 The British government agrees to Singapore governing itself. It joined the Federation of Malaysia in 1963 and became totally independent in 1965.

12

1961 SOVIET YURI ALEXEYEVICH GAGARIN BECOMES THE FIRST MAN IN SPACE.

The Soviets beat the Americans in the race to get the first man into space when Major Gagarin orbited the Earth for 108 minutes. He was in the space craft *Vostok* ('East'), travelling at more than 27,000 km/h (16,778 mph). US president John F. Kennedy congratulated the Soviets on their achievement. Gagarin had spent two years training for his trip and returned a national hero and international icon. The USSR had launched the world's first man-made satellite, *Sputnik*, in 1957 and later that same year, they sent a dog, Laika, into space.

13

1964 SIDNEY POITIER BECOMES THE FIRST BLACK ACTOR TO WIN AN OSCAR FOR BEST ACTOR.

An Oscar, the acting profession's top award, went to Sidney Poitier for his role in the movie *Lilies of the Field*. The only other black person to previously win an Oscar was Hattie McDaniel, who had been awarded the Best Supporting Actress award in 1939 for her role in *Gone with the Wind*.

Poitier grew up in poverty in the Bahamas in the Caribbean. Due to his strong Bahamian accent he was initially rejected by the American Negro Theatre in Harlem, New York. His first film was *No Way Out* in 1950 and his big breakthrough came five years later in *The Blackboard Jungle*.

In 2002 Denzel Washington and Halle Berry won the Best Actor and Best Actress Oscars, the first black actors to win since Poitier. At the same ceremony, Sidney Poitier was given a lifetime achievement award.

1997 Tiger Woods, 21, becomes the youngest player ever to win the US Masters Golf Championship.

41

14

1988 THE SOVIET UNION SIGNS AN AGREEMENT PLEDGING TO WITHDRAW ITS TROOPS FROM AFGHANISTAN.

The multi-ethnic Afghanistan lies along important trade routes connecting southern and eastern Asia to Europe and the Middle East. The pact was drawn up in negotiations between the United States, the USSR, Pakistan and Afghanistan. It ended nine years of occupation by the Soviet Union, which had intervened in 1979 to support the struggling communist government. The last Soviet troops left Afghanistan in February 1989 and a long period of civil war followed. The mujahideen overthrew President Najibullah in 1992 and the Pashtun-dominated Taliban seized control of the capital Kabul in 1996. The Taliban instituted a hardline version of Islam, banning women from work and introducing punishments such as amputation and stoning.

15

1998 FORMER CAMBODIAN DICTATOR, POL POT, DIES.
Pol Pot and the Khmer Rouge movement he led were behind the deaths of approximately 1.7 million Cambodians in the so-called 'killing fields' during the late 1970s. Pol Pot and his guerrilla soldiers came to power in 1975 after a war against the US-backed Cambodian government. Pot abolished money, private property and religion, and his troops forced people to leave the cities to set up rural collectives where many thousands died of disease and starvation. 'Intellectuals' were enemies of the new state and hundreds of thousands of the educated middle classes were tortured and executed. Pol Pot's radical reforms so weakened Cambodia that it was invaded by its old enemy, Vietnam, in 1979. The Khmer Rouge government fell and fled into the jungle. Vietnamese troops did not withdraw until 1989, leaving behind a country ravaged by civil war.

In 1991 a United Nations-brokered peace agreement was signed and led to free elections and the restoration of the monarchy in 1993. In 2001 Cambodia's senate approved a law to create a tribunal that would bring genocide charges against Khmer Rouge leaders.

1989 Ninety-six football fans are killed at the Hillsborough stadium in Sheffield, UK, during the FA Cup semi-final between Nottingham Forest and Liverpool.

16

1993 THE UNITED NATIONS MAKES THE BOSNIAN TOWN OF SREBRENICA A 'SAFE HAVEN' FOR BOSNIAN MUSLIM REFUGEES IN THE BOSNIAN WAR.
Under the United Nation's (UN) proposal, Srebrenica became a centre for Bosnian Muslim refugees seeking safety from Bosnian Serb aggressors. The designation of Srebrenica as a safe area was extended on 6 May to include five other Bosnian towns: Sarajevo, Tuzla, Zepa, Gorazde and Bihac.

The safe havens of Sarajevo and Gorazde were attacked by Bosnian Serbs in 1994, prompting UN air strikes. In 1995, Srebrenica was finally overrun by the Bosnian Serb forces of General Ratko Mladic. An estimated 7,000 Muslim men and boys were murdered and buried in mass graves in the worst atrocity in Europe since the Second World War. General Mladic was later indicted by the War Crimes Tribunal for genocide, but is still at large.

17

1961 A FORCE OF EXILED CUBANS INVADES CUBA AT THE BAY OF PIGS.
The invasion of Cuba was carried out from the sea and air by a force of about 1,400 exiled Cubans who had American support. They came ashore on an area of coast known as the Bay of Pigs, to the south-east of the capital, Havana. The invaders wanted to overthrow the country's communist leader, Fidel Castro. The leader of the

Cuban exile movement in the US was Dr Miro Cardona, who had been prime minister of Cuba for 45 days before Castro took over.

The fighting lasted just three days. More than 100 of the invaders died in the attack, and 1,189 were taken prisoner. Shortly afterwards, US President John F. Kennedy acknowledged US support for the invaders. The invasion strengthened Castro's hold on power, bringing the Soviet Union firmly on to his side. It acted as a key catalyst for the Cuban missile crisis 18 months later, on 28 October 1962, which brought the world to the brink of nuclear war.

1986 British journalist John McCarthy is kidnapped in the war-torn capital of Lebanon, Beirut. He is held hostage by militant group Islamic Jihad and is finally freed on 8 August 1991.

18

1955 ALBERT EINSTEIN DIES.
The eminent scientist and originator of the theory of relativity was born on 14 March 1879 to Jewish parents in Germany. His Special Theory of Relativity, which describes the motion of particles moving close to the speed of light, was published in 1905. His General Theory of Relativity was published in 1916 and in 1921 he was awarded the Nobel Prize for Physics.

Einstein's theories laid the groundwork for nuclear weapons and cosmic science. After his death, Einstein's brain was removed and studied by Canadian scientists. It was found that the part of Einstein's brain responsible for mathematical thought and the ability to think in terms of space and movement was 15 per cent wider than average.

19

2005 CARDINAL JOSEPH RATZINGER IS ELECTED POPE.
Following the death of Pope John Paul II, Cardinal Joseph Ratzinger was elected head of the world's 1.1 billion Roman Catholics. The 78-year-old German took the name Pope Benedict XVI. The 265th pontiff was a close friend of Pope John Paul II and was voted to succeed him by a group of 115 cardinals.

Pope Benedict XVI was born in 1927 in Bavaria, Germany. His seminary studies were interrupted by the Second World War and his supporters say that his experiences under the Nazi regime convinced him that the Church had to stand up for truth and freedom. Pope Benedict XVI is a conservative who firmly opposes birth control, supports the celibacy of priesthood and opposes the ordination of women.

20

1953 THE UNITED NATIONS AND KOREA BEGIN AN EXCHANGE OF PRISONERS IN THE KOREAN WAR.
Following Japan's defeat in the Second World War, the Soviet Union and the US had split Korea along the 38th parallel, separating North and South Korea. The

Communist North invaded the South in June 1950 and a United Nations force drove the invaders back to the Chinese border. China entered the war and together with the North Koreans occupied the Korean capital, Seoul, in 1951. United Nations forces counter-attacked and by 1953 retook all territory south of the 38th parallel.

The Allies and Korea exchanged sick and wounded prisoners of war at Panmunjon. The Korean War ended with the signing of the armistice on 27 July to restore the 38th parallel as a border. But a peace deal has never been reached and American troops remain stationed in the area separating North and South Korea.

21

1945 THE SOVIET RED ARMY ENTERS THE GERMAN CAPITAL BERLIN.

When the Red Army approached the German capital from three directions, north, east and south-east, the Nazi minister of propaganda, Josef Goebbels, issued a statement saying Berlin would be defended to the last.

Hitler ordered a counter-attack but the Wehrmacht's 9th Army was cut off. The Red Army, meanwhile, pressed on into the heart of Berlin using tanks to force their way into the city. Hitler committed suicide in his bunker on 30 April. By 2 May the old German parliament building, the Reichstag, had fallen and Marshal Zhukov claimed the honour of being Berlin's conqueror.

The war in Europe officially came to an end on 8 May 1945 with Germany's unconditional surrender to the Allied Forces.

22

1915 POISON GAS IS RELEASED AS A CHEMICAL WEAPON DURING THE SECOND BATTLE OF YPRES DURING THE FIRST WORLD WAR.

The Second Battle of Ypres was the first time during the First World War that Germany used poison gas on a large scale on the Western Front, the armed frontier between lands controlled by Germany to the east and the Allies Britain and France to the west.

The German Army released 168 tonnes of chlorine gas over a 6.5-km (4-mile) front. Thousands of Allied troops died within minutes from asphyxiation following tissue damage to the lungs. Many more were blinded as the gas filled the trenches and exposed the fleeing troops to enemy fire. Both sides went on to develop more sophisticated gas weapons and protective measures as the war progressed.

23

1984 THE AIDS VIRUS IS DISCOVERED.

The discovery of the virus that was thought to cause Acquired Immune Deficiency Syndrome, known as AIDS, was hailed as a 'monumental breakthrough' in medical research. AIDS weakens the immune system to the point where everyday infections become life-threatening.

The virus was a variant of a known human cancer virus called HTLV-3. The HTLV-3 virus was discovered to be the same as the LAV virus and to avoid confusion, it was re-named HIV in 1987. HIV is present in the blood, sexual fluids and breast milk of people who are infected with the virus. It is passed on when these infected fluids get into another person's system.

An estimated 24 million people have died of AIDS and it has reached pandemic proportions in parts of southern Africa. No successful vaccine has yet been discovered, but a series of drugs have now been developed that can significantly prolong the lives of people who are HIV-positive.

24

1990 NASA LAUNCHES THE HUBBLE SPACE TELESCOPE INTO SPACE ON BOARD THE SPACE SHUTTLE *DISCOVERY*.

The Hubble space telescope was launched into orbit 611.5 km (380 miles) above the Earth. The telescope, the size of a railway carriage, had taken 20 years to build and operates from high above the atmosphere, avoiding the interference that limits ground-based telescopes. It was discovered that Hubble's mirror had been made flatter than it should be by just one-fiftieth of the width of a human hair and, in December 1993, a complex operation was launched to repair the Hubble telescope while it was in orbit.

Since the repair, Hubble has sent back a series of stunning photographs of deep space, which have revolutionised thinking about the Universe. The pictures of Jupiter following the impact of Comet Shoemaker-Levy 9 in 1994 are among the most famous Hubble images.

Between 2003 and 2004, Hubble was directed to a single spot in the sky to obtain the deepest-ever view of the Universe, the so-called Hubble Ultra Deep Field. It showed the first stars beginning to shine, shortly after the moment when the Universe was created 13.7 billion years ago.

45

25

1974 ARMY REBELS SEIZE CONTROL OF PORTUGAL.

Army rebels took control of Portugal in a coup ending nearly 50 years of dictatorship. The former deputy armed forces minister, General Spinola, received the surrender of the prime minister, Dr Marcello Caetano, who fled into exile to the Portuguese island of Madeira. The Movement of the Armed Forces (MFA) took control. It issued a proclamation appealing for calm and patriotism, and promised to restore civil liberties and hold general elections as soon as possible.

General Spinola and his troops received a hero's welcome from crowds, who gave them cigarettes, food, newspapers and carnations. The 25 April coup became known as the Carnation Revolution, ending the longest dictatorship in Europe, the Estado Novo. The new regime pushed through a rapid and hasty programme of decolonisation. General Spinola served briefly as interim president and was succeeded by General Francisco da Costa Gomes. Over the course of the next decade a stable two-party system was established. Caetano spent the rest of his life in exile in Brazil.

Freedom Day is now celebrated as a national holiday in Portugal on 25 April.

26

1962 THE FIRST US ROCKET, *RANGER IV*, LANDS ON THE MOON.

The American Moon rocket *Ranger IV* landed on the far side of the moon. It was the first time an American spacecraft had successfully reached the Moon, with the Russians achieving the first-ever lunar impact in 1959.

The *Ranger* rockets were a significant part of America's attempt to be the first to put a man on the Moon. The first six *Rangers* failed to send back images of the Moon, with some of them missing the Moon entirely. Finally, on 31 July 1964, *Ranger VII* sent back more than 4,000 images before crashing into the Moon's *Mare Cognitum* ('Known Sea'). The *Rangers* gave scientists a new understanding of the Moon's surface and helped pave the way for the next stage of American space exploration, the *Apollo* astronauts.

27

1961 THE WEST AFRICAN STATE OF SIERRA LEONE BECOMES INDEPENDENT.

Sierra Leone won independence after more than 150 years of British colonial rule. In 1967, the All Peoples' Congress (APC) came to power under Siaka Stevens, who became president in 1971, and in 1978 made the APC the sole legal party in Sierra Leone. In 1985, Major General Joseph Momoh was elected president after being selected as the sole candidate. His government was dogged by corruption, and he was overthrown in a coup led by Captain Valentine Strasser in 1992.

At the same time, a vicious war broke out in neighbouring Liberia, and Sierra Leone became involved. Ten years of fighting followed, marked by atrocities and punishments to terrorise civilians. Peace was finally achieved in early 2002, with the help of Britain, the former colonial power, and a large United Nations peacekeeping mission.

28

1986 THE SOVIET UNION ACKNOWLEDGES THE CHERNOBYL NUCLEAR POWER PLANT DISASTER.

The Chernobyl nuclear power plant in the Ukraine consisted of four nuclear reactors. Design flaws led to a power surge, causing massive explosions that blew the top off a reactor, leading to a massive discharge of radioactivity. Chernobyl remains the world's worst civil nuclear disaster, although estimates of the numbers affected vary tremendously. A report in 2005 by the Chernobyl Forum, including members of the World Health Organisation, the United Nations and the governments of neighbouring Belarus, the Russian Federation and Ukraine, concluded that fewer than 50 people, most of them workers at the plant, died as a result of exposure to radiation. It is estimated that up to 9,000 people could eventually die from radiation exposure. Greenpeace, the international environmental organisation, claims the figure could actually be over 90,000.

Chernobyl is one of the most radioactive spots on Earth and an official exclusion zone around the plant remains in place, extending for 30 km (19 miles).

1945 Italian dictator Benito Mussolini is arrested and executed.

29

1993 ANNOUNCEMENT IS MADE THAT MEMBERS OF THE PUBLIC WILL BE ALLOWED INSIDE BUCKINGHAM PALACE FOR THE FIRST TIME.
The Queen's London residence was opened to the public during August and September, when the queen was at her Scottish residence in Balmoral. The adult entrance fee of £8 did not include permission to view the queen's private apartments, which remained closed. The intention was to raise money to pay for 70 per cent of the £40 million cost of restoring Windsor Castle, damaged by fire in November 1992. Around 380,000 people visited the Palace in the first year and approximately 300,000 visitors continue to do so every year, making it one of London's top tourist attractions.

30

1952 THE DIARY OF ANNE FRANK IS PUBLISHED IN ENGLISH.
The young Anne Frank's diary gave a fascinating account of life in hiding in Nazi-occupied Holland during the Second World War. In July 1942 the Franks and four other Jews went into hiding in an annex of a house in central Amsterdam. The annex was raided by the Gestapo on 4 August 1944 and the eight occupants were sent to the Auschwitz and Bergen-Belsen concentration camps. Anne Frank died just before her sixteenth birthday in Bergen-Belsen in 1945.
Anne's entry for 12 July 1944, three weeks before her arrest, read:
'I hear the approaching thunder that, one day, will destroy us ... I feel the suffering of millions. And yet, when I look up into the sky, I somehow feel that everything will change for the better, that this cruelty too will end, that peace and tranquillity will return once more.'
The Diary of Anne Frank was translated into 50 languages and became one of the most popular books in the world. The apartment in Amsterdam where the family hid, No. 263 Prinsengracht, is now the Anne Frank museum.

1945 Nazi leader Adolf Hitler commits suicide with his wife, Eva Braun, in his bunker in Berlin.

47

May

1

1945 GERMANY ANNOUNCES THE DEATH OF THE GERMAN FÜHRER, ADOLF HITLER.

Adolf Hitler was the military and political leader of Germany from 1933. Born on 20 April 1889 in Braunau-am-Inn on the Austrian-German border, he fought in the German Army during the First World War. In 1919 he joined the fascist German Workers' Party (DAP), promising extremist solutions to Germany's post-war economic problems.

By 1921 Hitler was the leader of what had become the National Socialist German Workers' Party (NSDAP or Nazi Party). Against a background of economic depression and political turmoil, the Nazis became the largest party in the German parliament in the 1932 elections and in January 1933 Hitler became chancellor of a coalition government.

He quickly passed extreme anti-Jewish laws and embarked on a policy of territorial expansion that eventually led to the Second World War.

The first details about the real circumstances of Hitler's death became known on 20 June. He had committed suicide with his wife of one day, Eva Braun. Their partly burned bodies were discovered near the entrance of his bunker at the Reich Chancery.

Germany signed an unconditional surrender to the Allies on 7 May, and the Second World War ended in Europe on 8 May.

1994 Brazilian racing driver and winner of 41 Grands Prix, Ayrton Senna, is killed in a car crash at the San Marino Grand Prix.

2

1997 THE LABOUR PARTY WINS A LANDSLIDE VICTORY AGAINST THE CONSERVATIVES IN THE UK GENERAL ELECTION.

Labour won its largest number of seats in the history of the party, with 419 seats against the Conservatives' 165. Labour leader Tony Blair, aged 43, became the youngest British prime minister of the twentieth century. A record 120 women were voted into parliament and there were an unprecedented five women in Blair's first cabinet. Following the Tory defeat, Conservative leader John Major resigned and was succeeded by William Hague.

Labour won the general election again in 2001 and on 5 May 2005 Blair secured an historic third term for Labour. However, following Britain's involvement in the unpopular war in Iraq, the party's majority was drastically reduced. Tony Blair resigned as prime minister on 27 June 2007 and was succeeded by his former chancellor, Gordon Brown.

3

1968 SURGEONS CONDUCT BRITAIN'S FIRST HUMAN HEART TRANSPLANT.
Britain's first heart transplant was successfully carried out by a team of 18 doctors and nurses at the National Heart Hospital in Marylebone, London. The operation took more than seven hours to complete. Britain's first heart transplant patient, who was later named as Frederick West, died from an infection 46 days after receiving the donor heart. British surgeons had a cautious approach to heart surgery over the next decade, and only six more transplants were carried out. By the 1980s, heart transplants had become more common and today around 300 heart transplant operations are carried out in the UK every year. In 1984 Britain's first successful heart-lung transplant was carried out.

The first heart transplant ever was carried out by Christian Barnard in South Africa in 1967.

4

1979 THE CONSERVATIVE PARTY WINS THE GENERAL ELECTION AND MARGARET THATCHER BECOMES BRITAIN'S FIRST WOMAN PRIME MINISTER.
Margaret Thatcher arrived at Downing Street to take over from Labour's James Callaghan, after her party won an overall majority of 43 seats, quoting St Francis of Assisi:

'Where there is discord, may we bring harmony.'

Thatcher, dubbed the 'Iron Lady', was one of the dominant political figures of the twentieth century. Born in 1925 in Grantham, Lincolnshire, she famously needed only four hours' sleep a night during her 11 years as Conservative leader. Her strong leadership style was demonstrated during the 1982 Falklands War, which led to a landslide Conservative victory in the 1983 election. In 1984, she narrowly escaped death when the IRA planted a bomb at the Conservative Party conference in Brighton. Her opposition to the idea of Britain joining the European Union led to disputes within the Conservative Party and in 1990 she was replaced as leader of the Conservatives by John Major. The Conservative Party remained in power until Labour's historic victory in 1997.

In 1992 Thatcher left the House of Commons for the House of Lords, as Baroness Thatcher of Kesteven.

5

1967 THE FIRST ALL-BRITISH SATELLITE, *ARIEL 3*, IS LAUNCHED INTO ORBIT.
Ariel 3 was propelled into space from Vandenberg Air Force Base in California. The project was the result of close cooperation between the British Science Research Council and NASA. The small satellite was sent to survey the ionospheric conditions about 60 km (37 miles) above the Earth's surface. It initially orbited the Earth every

95 minutes and relayed information back to a computer at Slough's Radio and Space Research Station in the UK. Since the 1960s, hundreds of satellites have been launched into orbit for weather forecasting, navigation, communications and monitoring the Earth for the effects of global warming.

1961 Alan Shepard becomes the first US astronaut in space, three weeks after Russian cosmonaut Yuri Gagarin became the first man in space.

6

1994 THE CHANNEL TUNNEL OPENS BETWEEN BRITAIN AND FRANCE.

The Channel Tunnel was the first land link between Britain and Europe since the last ice age, 8,000 years previously. It had taken eight years to complete, at a cost of £10 billion. The queen and France's president François Mitterrand formally opened the Channel Tunnel. The tunnel is 50 km (31 miles) long, of which 37 km (23 miles) are under the sea. The average depth under the seabed is 45 m (148 ft). It takes 20 minutes to make the crossing by rail with Eurostar, and the London to Paris journey time is two hours 15 minutes.

1954 Roger Bannister becomes the first man to run a mile in under four minutes, with a time of 3 minutes and 59.4 seconds.

7

1956 THE BRITISH HEALTH MINISTER REJECTS CALLS FOR A GOVERNMENT CAMPAIGN AGAINST SMOKING.

The health minister R. H. Turton rejected calls for a government campaign against smoking, saying no ill-effects had actually been proven. This was despite the fact that two cancer-causing agents had been identified in tobacco smoke. In June 1957 the UK government accepted the 'causal relationship' between tobacco and cancer, and in March 1962 the Royal College of Physicians issued the first of four landmark reports linking cigarettes with fatal disease.

The tobacco industry in the USA and UK continued to deny the link between cancer and smoking for decades, but in 1965 health warnings appeared for the first time on cigarette packets in the USA. Cigarette manufacturers in the UK followed suit in 1971. It has since been proven that as well as cancer, smoking also causes heart disease, lung disease, asthma and premature ageing. It is estimated that one in five deaths in the UK are from a smoking-related illness.

8

1945 GERMANY SIGNS AN UNCONDITIONAL SURRENDER, ENDING THE SECOND WORLD WAR IN EUROPE.

Simultaneous broadcasts officially announcing the end of war in Europe went out in London, Washington and Moscow. The British prime minister, Winston Churchill, made a broadcast to the nation from 10 Downing Street, London, followed by a statement in the Commons. Huge crowds, many dressed in red, white and blue, gathered outside Buckingham Palace in London to celebrate. In his speech he said:

'In the long years to come not only will the people of this island but of the world, wherever the bird of freedom chirps in human hearts, look back to what we've done and they will say "do not despair, do not yield to violence and tyranny, march straightforward and die if need be-unconquered."'

In Britain, 8 May was declared a national holiday to mark Victory in Europe Day, or VE Day. The war against Japan continued for another four months, with that country's final surrender on 14 August.

9

1955 WEST GERMANY JOINS THE NORTH ATLANTIC TREATY ORGANISATION (NATO).

Ministers from 14 member countries, including British foreign secretary Harold Macmillan, welcomed West Germany into NATO.

At the end of the Second World War, Germany had been split by the Allied nations at the Potsdam Conference in August 1945 in order to prevent another attempt by Germany to take over Europe. West Germany was reunified with East Germany on 3 October 1990. The USSR saw West Germany's inclusion into NATO as a direct threat and in the same year, it created the Warsaw Pact. This counter-alliance dissolved after the break-up of the USSR in 1991. NATO formed closer links with former Eastern Bloc countries by setting up a North Atlantic Cooperation Council in 1991 and the Partnership for Peace programme in 1994.

The Czech Republic, Hungary and Poland became the first former Warsaw Pact countries to gain NATO membership in 1999.

51

10

1994 NELSON MANDELA BECOMES SOUTH AFRICA'S FIRST BLACK PRESIDENT.

Nelson Mandela became South Africa's first black president after more than three centuries of white rule. Mandela's African National Congress (ANC) party won 252 of the 400 seats in the first democratic elections of South Africa's history. Mandela pledged:

'Never, never again will this beautiful land experience the oppression of one by another.'

Born in 1918, Mandela was an anti-apartheid activist who spent 27 years in prison for opposing the reigning white regime in South Africa. As president, Mandela entrusted his deputy, Thabo Mbeki, with the day-to-day business of the government while he himself concentrated on building a new international image for South Africa. Mandela stepped down as South Africa's president after the ANC's landslide victory in the national elections in the summer of 1999, in favour of Mr Mbeki. He remains a cultural icon of freedom and equality and won the Nobel Peace Prize in 1993.

11

1998 INDIA ANNOUNCES IT HAS CARRIED OUT A SERIES OF UNDERGROUND NUCLEAR TESTS.

The experiments, the first in India since 1974, took place without any warning to the international community. There was widespread concern, with the United States and several other countries imposing economic sanctions on India in response to the move.

The test site, in Pokhran in the desert state of Rajasthan, is only about 150 km (93 miles) from the Indian border with Pakistan. The two countries had fought three wars since gaining independence from Britain in 1947, mainly over the disputed territories of Jammu and Kashmir, and there were fears that the tests could trigger a regional nuclear arms race. Pakistan did retaliate on 28 May, by conducting its own nuclear tests.

In February 1999, India and Pakistan signed the Lahore accord, pledging to 'resolve all issues', including that of Jammu and Kashmir, but hostilities over Kashmir broke out again within three months.

12

2000 FORD ENDS MORE THAN 70 YEARS OF CAR PRODUCTION AT ITS DAGENHAM PLANT IN ESSEX.

For more than 70 years, the Dagenham plant, one of Europe's first major car-assembly sites, was regarded as a focal point of the UK car industry. Ford's European operations had been hit by falling car sales and intense competition. The last Ford Fiesta came off the production line in Dagenham in February 2002 and the factory was downsized to produce engines and gearboxes. Car production was moved to Ford's German factory in Cologne, with a loss of over 2,000 jobs at Dagenham.

13

1981 POPE JOHN PAUL II IS SHOT IN ROME.

Pope John Paul II was shot as he blessed the crowds in St Peter's Square in Rome. The pope was being driven in his popemobile when he was struck by four bullets. Surgeons performed a five-hour operation on him and the pope eventually made a full recovery.

Turkish Mehmet Ali Agca was sentenced to life imprisonment in July 1981 for the shooting. The pope later publicly forgave Agca and in June 2000, with the agreement of the pope himself, Agca was pardoned by the Italian president after serving 19 years.

Pope John Paul II died on 2 April 2005.

1995 Alison Hargreaves becomes the first woman to conquer Mount Everest, the world's highest mountain, unaided.

14

1955 THE SOVIET UNION AND ITS EASTERN BLOC ALLIES SIGN THE WARSAW PACT.
The Soviet Union and its seven Eastern Bloc allies – Poland, East Germany, Czechoslovakia, Hungary, Romania, Bulgaria and Albania – signed a security pact in the Polish capital, Warsaw. It was designed to ensure close integration of military, economic and cultural policy between the eight communist nations following the perceived threat of West Germany joining the western nations in the North Atlantic Treaty Organisation (NATO). Members of the Pact placed their armed forces under the command of Marshal Koniev.

The Warsaw Pact permitted the Soviet Union to suppress nationalist rebellions. The Soviet Union went on to crush uprisings in Hungary in 1956 and Czechoslovakia in 1968. The democratic revolutions of 1989 in Eastern Europe marked the end of the Cold War between East and West. East Germany withdrew from the Pact in 1990 and, on 1 July 1991, it was declared 'non-existent'.

15

1957 BRITAIN DROPS ITS FIRST HYDROGEN BOMB.
After two years of development, Britain exploded its first H-Bomb at high altitude over the largely uninhabited Christmas Island in the Pacific Ocean. The bomb was part of the British thermo-nuclear weapons programme to develop the megaton hydrogen bomb, which was as powerful as one million tonnes of TNT. The tests raised a major debate about the dangers of nuclear weapons and an arms race between the political superpowers in the East and the West. It resulted in the founding of the Campaign for Nuclear Disarmament (CND) in 1958, which pressed for international abandonment of nuclear weapons. In 1963, the Soviet Union, the UK, the USA and many other countries agreed to a Nuclear Test Ban Treaty.

The Valiant aircraft XD818 that dropped the first British H-Bomb is now in the RAF Museum at Hendon.

53

16

1943 THE GERMAN ARMY CRUSHES AN UPRISING IN THE JEWISH GHETTO IN WARSAW, POLAND.
The Nazis created the Jewish ghetto in German-occupied Poland in 1940. Approximately 500,000 men, women and children were crammed into an area of 2.6 sq km (1 sq mile). Its inhabitants were routinely transported to the Treblinka death camp. The uprising began on 19 April when SS troops entered the ghetto in tanks to take Jews to the railway station for transportation to concentration camps. The SS were attacked by Jews using homemade explosives, rifles, small arms and even a light machine-gun.

Jewish men and women valiantly fought the German troops for 28 days, until local SS Commander Brigadier Stroop ordered the demolition of the entire Jewish ghetto.

Around 40,000 Jews were massacred in retaliation for the uprising. When Soviet troops liberated Warsaw on 17 January 1945, the old city had been virtually destroyed and only around 200 Jews had survived. One of these was Jewish-Polish pianist and composer Wladyslaw Szpilman, whose autobiograhical book *The Pianist* recounts his incredible experience.

17

2000 TWO ROYAL MARINE COMMANDOS ARE THE FIRST BRITONS TO REACH THE NORTH POLE UNAIDED.

Corporal Alan Chambers and marine Charlie Paton were the first Britons to reach the geographical North Pole without outside support. They spent 67 days dragging sledges of supplies 1,127 km (700 miles) across the ice to get to the geographical North Pole, where temperatures reached as low as –30°C (–22°F).

In June 2002 Ann Daniels and Caroline Hamilton finished their hike to the North Pole to become the first women to walk to both poles, having reached the South Pole five months earlier.

18

1991 HELEN SHARMAN BECOMES BRITAIN'S FIRST ASTRONAUT IN SPACE.

The 27-year-old Helen Sharman was on board the Soviet *Soyuz TM-12* space capsule with fellow cosmonauts Anatoly Artebartsky and Sergei Krikalyov. Sharman had won her place in space in 1989 after answering an advertisement she heard on the car radio:

'Astronaut wanted. No experience necessary.'

She was selected from more than 13,000 applicants to be the British member of the Russian scientific space mission, Project Juno, and spent 18 months in training for her mission to land on the Mir space station. Seven days later Sharman came back to Earth in her *Soyuz TM-11* capsule, which parachuted into Kazakhstan.

Helen Sharman was awarded an OBE in 1993 and has since become a lecturer and broadcaster on science education.

19

1980 MOUNT ST HELENS VOLCANO IN THE USA ERUPTS, KILLING 57 PEOPLE.

When Mount St Helens in Washington State erupted it triggered an earthquake measuring 5.2 on the Richter scale. The north face of the mountain collapsed in a massive avalanche at the same time as a giant mushroom-shaped cloud of ash rose 24 km (15 miles) into the sky. Avalanches of hot ash, pumice and gas rushed out of the volcanic crater. The explosion was the largest in US history, and was as powerful as 500 atomic bombs exploding.

Fifty-seven people died, with nearly 7,000 deer, elk and bears perishing, as well as birds and small mammals. According to the US Department of Agriculture, out of 32 species of small mammals thought to be living near Mount St Helens, only 14 were known to have survived.

The volcano became active again in October 2004, but scientists believe the chances of an imminent eruption as massive as that in 1980 are low.

20

1932 AMELIA EARHART BEGINS THE FIRST NON-STOP SOLO FLIGHT ACROSS THE ATLANTIC BY A FEMALE PILOT.

Born in 1897 in Kansas, USA, Amelia Earhart was an aviation pioneer and women's rights advocate. On 20 May 1932 she set off from Harbour Grace, Newfoundland to fly across the Atlantic in her single-engine Lockheed Vega. After a flight lasting just under 15 hours, she landed at Culmore, Northern Ireland. As the first woman to fly solo non-stop across the Atlantic, Earhart was awarded the Distinguished Flying Cross. She disappeared over the central Pacific Ocean during an attempt to make a circumnavigational flight in 1937.

21

1991 RAJIV GANDHI, THE FORMER INDIAN PRIME MINISTER, IS ASSASSINATED.

Gandhi was campaigning for the Congress Party during the world's largest democratic election when a bomb exploded, killing him instantly. It emerged that a female Tamil Tiger suicide bomber had assassinated Rajiv Gandhi. The Liberation Tigers of Tamil Eelam (LTTE) were a violent guerrilla group fighting for a separate homeland for Tamils on the island of Sri Lanka. They had resented Gandhi's attempts, when as prime minister in 1987 he had tried to impose peace in the country.

Gandhi's death marked the end of the Nehru dynasty that had led India for all but five years since independence from Britain in 1947. He became prime minister after his mother, Indira Gandhi, was assassinated by her own Sikh bodyguards in 1984.

22

1939 GERMANY AND ITALY SIGN THE PACT OF STEEL.

The Pact of Steel, formally known as the Pact of Friendship and Alliance between Germany and Italy, was an agreement between fascist Italy and Nazi Germany. It signified an open declaration of cooperation between the two countries, while a 'Secret Supplementary Protocol' encouraged a joint military and economic policy.

The pact obliged Italy to join the Second World War as Germany's ally after Adolf Hitler's invasion of Poland in 1939, but Italy did not actually enter the war until June 1940. Italy's surrender and subsequent alliance with the Western Allies of the Second World War in 1943 effectively ended the pact.

23

1998 THE GOOD FRIDAY AGREEMENT IS OVERWHELMINGLY ACCEPTED IN A REFERENDUM IN NORTHERN IRELAND.
The Good Friday Agreement was a major political development in the Northern Ireland peace process. It was signed in Belfast by the British and Irish governments on 10 April 1998 (Good Friday), and endorsed by most Northern Ireland political parties. The voters of Northern Ireland and the Republic of Ireland endorsed it in separate referendums.

One of the agreement's main principles was for a devolved Northern Ireland Assembly, free from the rule of the British parliament. Direct rule finally ended in May 2007, when the Northern Ireland Assembly met with the return of devolution and Democratic Unionist Party leader Ian Paisley as first minister. The deputy first minister is the Irish Republican Martin McGuinness.

1949 The Federal Republic of Germany, commonly known as West Germany, is established.

24

1975 JOURNALISTS LEAVE SAIGON, SOUTH VIETNAM.
A group of 80 journalists were the first westerners to be allowed to leave the capital of South Vietnam since its capture by communist forces on 29 April. The journalists boarded a Russian-made plane belonging to the North Vietnamese Air Force and departed for Vientiane in Laos, the only Indo-Chinese country that still had diplomatic ties with the United States.

The fall of Saigon was celebrated by victory parades by the communist forces. The event marked the end of the war in Vietnam, which had been raging for three decades, with communists fighting the colonial power, France, and then the US-backed South Vietnam.

1915 Italy enters the First World War on the side of the Allies and declares war on Austria-Hungary.

25

1963 THIRTY-TWO AFRICAN STATES UNITE AGAINST WHITE RULE IN AFRICA.
Leaders of 32 African nations founded the Organisation of African Unity (OAU). The organisation was to be based in Addis Ababa, the Ethiopian capital. The primary aim of the OAU, which represented a population of 200 million, was to 'decolonise' British-ruled states in southern Rhodesia, South Africa, Mozambique and Angola.

During the 1970s, the OAU provided support for the liberation movements in various countries, including Zimbabwe and Mozambique. During the 1980s, it put pressure on countries in the West to impose sanctions on South Africa for its apartheid movement.

On 25 May 2001, 38 years after it was founded, the OAU was dissolved and was replaced by the African Union, which aims to unify the 53 African member states politically, socially and economically.

1967 Jock Stein's Glasgow Celtic defeats Internacionale Milan to become the first British football team to win the European Cup.

26

1998 JAPANESE EMPEROR AKIHITO SPEAKS OF HIS 'DEEP SORROW' OVER THE SUFFERING CAUSED BY JAPANESE PRISONER-OF-WAR CAMPS DURING THE SECOND WORLD WAR.

The Japanese had taken 50,016 British military personnel captive during the war, and of these, 12,433 died or had been killed in captivity, where they endured enormous cruelty and hardship. Addressing a state banquet attended by the queen, Emperor Akihito of Japan spoke of his 'deep sorrow and pain' over the suffering inflicted by Japan.

In 2000, the British government granted a total of £100 million to 16,700 former prisoners of war (POWs) or their widows. The chairman of the Japanese Labour Camp Survivors' Association said the veterans would continue to seek a full apology from the Japanese emperor.

27

1964 JAWAHARLAL NEHRU, FOUNDER OF MODERN INDIA AND ITS CURRENT PRIME MINISTER, DIES.

Jawaharlal Nehru had become India's first prime minister in 1947. Nearly 250,000 men, women and children filed past his body to pay their respects to the man honoured as the architect of modern India.

The son of a lawyer, Nehru was a key figure in the struggle for Indian independence. He was a confidant of Independence leader Mahatma Gandhi, and was imprisoned several times in the fight to break away from British rule. Although some of his policies during his 17 years in power have been discredited in recent years, Nehru remains a legendary and much-loved figure in India's early history.

Lal Shastri succeeded Nehru, but served for less than two years. He was succeeded by Nehru's daughter, Indira Gandhi. This began the long Nehru-Gandhi dynasty that has dominated Indian politics to this day.

28

1959 TWO MONKEYS BECOME THE FIRST LIVING CREATURES TO SURVIVE A FLIGHT IN SPACE.
The two monkeys – Able, a female rhesus monkey, and Baker, a female squirrel monkey – were fired into space in a Jupiter missile AM-18 from Cape Canaveral in Florida in the United States.

Their flight reached speeds of up to 16,000 km/h (10,000 mph) and lasted for 15 minutes. In space, the monkeys were weightless for nine minutes. They were monitored throughout the flight for changes in their heartbeats, muscular reaction, pulse velocity, body temperature and rate of breathing.

Although the mission was seen as a success by space experts, it was criticised by animal welfare groups.

29

1953 EDMUND HILLARY AND TENZING NORGAY BECOME THE FIRST EXPLORERS TO REACH THE SUMMIT OF MOUNT EVEREST.
New Zealander Edmund Hillary and Nepalese Sherpa Tenzing Norgay reached the top of the highest summit in the world after a gruelling climb up the southern face. The peak is 8,847 m (29,025 ft) above sea level.

Edmund Hillary was knighted on his return to England. He took part in several more major expeditions, including a trip across Antarctica to the South Pole in 1958. Tenzing Norgay was awarded the George Medal and later became director of the Himalayan Mountaineering Institute. He died in 1986.

By the fiftieth anniversary of the historic ascent in May 2003 more than 1,300 people had reached the summit of Mount Everest.

1968 Manchester United becomes the first English football club to win the European Cup.

30

1981 PRESIDENT OF BANGLADESH, ZIA RAHMAN, IS ASSASSINATED BY THE MILITARY.
The president of Bangladesh, Zia Rahman, was assassinated in the south-eastern city of Chittagong. He was killed by sub-machine-gun bullets when he opened the door of his house to see what was happening outside. Eight people died in the shooting, including a security officer, an officer who was guarding the president, and one of the attackers.

The killing was believed to be part of a rebellion by a faction within the Bangladeshi military. The army, under its chief of staff, Major General Hussain Muhammad Ershad, remained loyal to the Dhaka government and quickly put down the rebellion.

Army officers had been involved in several attempts to remove President Zia from office during his six-year rule.

In the capital Dhaka, tens of thousands of people took to the streets to show their grief at the death of their president, who was widely admired and respected.

1911 The first Indianapolis 500 automobile race is run in Indianapolis, Indiana, United States.

31

1985 THE FOOTBALL ASSOCIATION BANS ENGLISH FOOTBALL CLUBS FROM PLAYING IN EUROPE FOLLOWING THE HEYSEL STADIUM TRAGEDY IN BELGIUM.

The Football Association banned English clubs from playing in Europe following the Heysel stadium tragedy on 29 May. Thirty-nine people died and more than 400 were injured when a wall collapsed at the stadium in Brussels during violent riots before the start of the European Cup final between Liverpool and Juventus (Turin). Most of the victims were Italian. The ban was lifted in 1990 and violence in football grounds has been reduced due to closed-circuit TV, seating in stadiums, segregation of rival fans and the banning of alcohol.

June

1

1979 WHITE MINORITY RULE ENDS IN RHODESIA AFTER NEARLY 90 YEARS.

Under a new black prime minister, Bishop Murorewa, the African state of Rhodesia declared its independence from British rule and its new name of Zimbabwe-Rhodesia. The state of Zimbabwe-Rhodesia did not receive international recognition and lasted just over six months before the country became a British colony again.

Zimbabwe became an official, internationally recognised republic on 18 April 1980, when the Zimbabwe African National Union (ZANU), led by Robert Mugabe, won the general election. President Mugabe supported the violent campaign to seize white-owned farms in 2000, and the European Union imposed sanctions on Zimbabwe in 2002. Mugabe was re-elected as president in 2002, amid widespread claims of intimidation in a country suffering from economic collapse and mass starvation.

2

1953 QUEEN ELIZABETH II IS CROWNED AT WESTMINSTER ABBEY.

Queen Elizabeth II was crowned at a coronation ceremony in Westminster Abbey in London. Over 8,000 guests, including prime ministers and heads of state from around the Commonwealth attended. Twenty million people around the world watched the ceremony as the BBC provided live coverage of the event on radio and television in 44 languages. Queen Elizabeth, aged 25, replaced her father, King George VI, as monarch following his death on 6 February 1952. In 2002 she celebrated her Golden Jubilee.

3

1965 EDWARD WHITE BECOMES THE FIRST AMERICAN TO WALK IN SPACE.

Far above the Earth (193 km/120 miles), Major Edward Higgins White II opened the hatch of the *Gemini 4* spacecraft and stepped out of the capsule, becoming the first American astronaut to walk in space. White was attached to the craft by a 7.6-m (25-ft) tether and controlled his movements with a hand-held oxygen jet-propulsion gun. He remained outside the capsule for just over 20 minutes. Two years later White was killed along with two other astronauts when *Apollo 1* caught fire on the launchpad. As a space walker, White had been preceded by Soviet cosmonaut Aleksei A. Leonov, who on 18 March 1965 became the first man ever to walk in space.

1937 Edward VIII marries American divorcee Wallis Simpson at the Chateau de Cande in France. His decision leads to the British abdication crisis.

4

1989 CHINESE ARMY MASSACRES CIVILIANS IN TIANANMEN SQUARE. Hundreds, possibly thousands of civilians were shot dead by the Chinese Army during a military operation to crush a democratic protest in China's capital, Peking (now more widely known as Beijing). The army moved tanks in to the square to disperse protestors and then fired at the unarmed demonstrators. The protests had begun seven weeks before with a march by students in memory of former party leader Hu Yaobang. Millions of people from all walks of life joined in their demonstration and their demands for democratic reform have since been described as the greatest challenge to the communist state in China since the 1949 revolution.

It has been suggested that the communist leader Deng Xiaoping personally ordered the military's involvement. The attack on unarmed civilians brought condemnation from around the world.

1940 The British evacuation of Allied troops at Dunkirk, codenamed Operation Dynamo, ends.

5

1944 ALLIED TROOPS LIBERATE ROME FROM THE GERMAN ARMY. Italy entered the Second World War in June 1940 as a German ally, with fascist prime minister Benito Mussolini hoping to establish a new Italian empire in North Africa. The Allied troops first invaded mainland Italy at the beginning of September 1943 and Italy surrendered on 8 September 1943. After the fall of Rome in 1944, German forces fell back to the so-called Gothic Line of defence. This ran across Italy just north of Florence and the Allies did not breach this line of defence until September 1944. Eventual victory in Europe was won only through direct attacks on Germany itself, leading to unconditional surrender on 8 May 1945.

1967 Start of the six-day Arab-Israeli War between Syria and Israel.

6

1944 D-DAY IN EUROPE, WITH THE ALLIED TROOPS' NORMANDY LANDINGS. Thousands of Allied troops began landing on the beaches of Normandy in northern France at the start of a major offensive to liberate German-occupied Europe during the Second World War.

The Normandy landings were the beginning of Operation Overlord and were preceded by air attacks along the French coast. The invasion of Normandy was the largest assault of its kind ever launched. It involved five army divisions in the initial assault and more than 7,000 ships. In addition, 11,000 aircraft were involved. In total 75,215 British and Canadian troops and 57,500 US troops were landed by sea on D-Day. Another 23,400 were landed by air.

To keep the landings destination secret, a deception plan, Operation Fortitude, was mounted, leading the Germans to believe that the main target was further east along the coast at Pas de Calais. The tactic worked because when the landings finally began, there were only 14 German divisions waiting to face the Allies. The end of the Normandy campaign came with the destruction of the German 7th Army in August.

1975 British voters back the UK's continued membership of the European Economic Community (EEC) by a large majority in a nationwide referendum.

7

1977 QUEEN ELIZABETH II CELEBRATES HER SILVER JUBILEE.
More than one million people lined the streets of London to watch the royal family on its way to St Paul's Cathedral at the start of the queen's Silver Jubilee celebrations. The queen, accompanied by her husband Prince Philip, led the procession in the golden state coach. Later the royal family appeared on the balcony of Buckingham Palace.

Across Britain, millions of people tuned in to watch the events on the television and many more celebrated with their own street parties. While the celebrations were taking place, punk band the Sex Pistols sailed down the Thames playing their controversial version of 'God Save the Queen'. They were arrested as they came ashore.

The queen toured Britain and the Commonwealth throughout 2002, the year of her Golden Jubilee.

8

1982 A SURPRISE ARGENTINE AIR ATTACK DURING THE FALKLANDS WAR LEADS TO BRITISH CASUALTIES.
On 2 April 1982, Argentina invaded the Falkland Islands, a British colony in the South Atlantic. The Argentines said it was a bid to reclaim sovereignty of the islands that they had inherited from Spain in the 1800s. British prime minister Margaret Thatcher quickly chose to fight to defend the remote British colony, which Britain had ruled for 150 years. Seven weeks after the Argentines invaded, the first major British troop landing began on the islands at San Carlos on 21 May.

The surprise Argentine air attack on two British supply ships on 8 June claimed 48 lives. *Sir Galahad* and *Sir Tristram* were anchored off Fitzroy in Port Pleasant, near Bluff Cove, when they were bombed in a surprise raid by five Argentine Skyhawks in what became known as the Battle of Bluff Cove. The Argentines surrendered to the British on 14 June. During the short, bitter conflict, 655 Argentine servicemen, 255 British servicemen and three Falkland islanders were killed.

9

1975 THE FIRST LIVE TRANSMISSION FROM THE BRITISH HOUSES OF PARLIAMENT IS BROADCAST.
The House of Commons is a democratically elected body, consisting of 646 members, who are known as members of parliament, or MPs. The first live transmission from the Commons was broadcast by BBC Radio and commercial stations. Secretary of state for industry Tony Benn was the first minister to be questioned in parliament live on air. In November 1984, cameras were installed in the House of Lords, the upper house of parliament for an experimental period, and have remained there since. After an 18-month trial, permission was granted for television broadcasts in the House of Commons in 1990.

1983 Margaret Thatcher's Conservative Party wins a landslide second-term election victory in Britain.

10

1967 END OF THE SIX-DAY WAR BETWEEN ISRAEL AND SYRIA.
Fighting in the Middle East ended after Israel finally observed the United Nations' ceasefire and halted its advance into Syria. Within the previous six days Israeli troops had taken territory many times larger than Israel itself and united the holy city of Jerusalem for the first time since 1948. Israeli prime minister Levi Eshkol said his country was acting in self-defence.

63

The Arab-Israeli war displaced around 500,000 Palestinians, who fled to Egypt, Syria, Lebanon and Jordan. In November 1967, the UN Security Council adopted Resolution 242. This stated that Israel must withdraw from territories occupied in the war in exchange for peace with its neighbours. This resolution has formed the basis of all Arab-Israeli negotiations since.

1910 American blues singer and composer Howlin' Wolf, one of the most famous urban blues musicians, is born in West Point, Mississippi, USA.

11

1959 THE HOVERCRAFT IS LAUNCHED.
The hovercraft was a revolutionary new form of transport that could operate on sea and land. It was invented by boat-builder Christopher Cockerell, and was propelled on a cushion of air hovering just above the waves to reduce the amount of friction felt as it travelled through water. The first hovercraft, the SRN-1 could reach speeds of up to 25 knots.
More than 80 million people and 12 million cars have since crossed the English Channel by hovercraft. The cross-channel service was stopped in October 2000 because of increased competition from ferries and the Channel Tunnel.

12

1964 AFRICAN NATIONAL CONGRESS LEADER NELSON MANDELA IS JAILED FOR LIFE.

Nelson Mandela, leader of the anti-apartheid struggle in South Africa, was jailed for life for sabotage. Seven other defendants, including the former secretary-general of the banned African National Congress (ANC), Walter Sisulu, were also given life prison sentences. The Rivonia trial, as it was called, had begun eight months before, with Mandela admitting to plotting to destroy the South African state by sabotage in a bid to end the oppression of black South Africans.

Mandela spent most of his 27 years in prison serving hard labour in Robben Island prison off the South African coast near Cape Town. He was released on 11 February 1990 and in 1994 became South Africa's first democratically elected president in the country's first multi-racial elections. He stepped down as president in 1999, but continues to travel the world campaigning for peace.

13

1991 BORIS YELTSIN WINS THE FIRST RUSSIAN ELECTIONS.

Boris Yeltsin became the country's first elected president, defeating the Communist Party, which had ruled since the 1917 Russian Revolution.

Yeltsin became head of three-quarters of the Soviet landmass and 150 million people. President Mikhail Gorbachev remained president of the Soviet Union, but in August 1991 Soviet hardliners staged a coup against him and President Yeltsin emerged as a national hero who had tried to keep the peace. Gorbachev stepped down as Soviet leader on 25 December 1991 and Yeltsin became president of independent Russia. He pushed ahead with a radical programme of reforms but stepped down as president on 1 January 2000 when parliament forced him to accept limitations on his powers.

14

1940 GERMAN TROOPS TAKE PARIS DURING THE SECOND WORLD WAR.

Adolf Hitler's attack on Western Europe began on 10 May, when the Germans carried out air raids on Belgium and Holland. They took northern France despite heavy resistance from Allied forces. When German troops marched into the French capital city, French and Allied forces retreated without resistance to avoid the total destruction of the city.

On 17 June, Henri-Philippe Pétain became the new French premier. Pétain negotiated an armistice, which was signed on 22 June. French Resistance movements fought the Nazi occupiers as well as the Vichy regime headed by Pétain, which collaborated with the Nazis. The liberation of Paris from the Germans took place in Paris between 19 and 25 August 1944.

1982 Ceasefire agreed between British and Argentine forces in the Falklands War.

15

2000 BRITISH MILITARY TASK FORCE LEAVES SIERRA LEONE.
Britain, the former colonial power in Sierra Leone, handed responsibility for security in the war-torn West African state over to the United Nations (UN). British troops had entered Sierra Leone after a peace deal between government and rebel forces had broken down. Rebels were defeating the Sierra Leone Army and the UN peacekeeping force in a bitter civil war. After six weeks, the British military withdrew, leaving a core team of 300 soldiers to train the demoralised Sierra Leone Army.

Sierra Leone's civil war resulted in more than two million of the country's 4.5 million population being displaced. At least 50,000 people died in the fighting and there were an estimated 100,000 victims of mutilation. The economy was left in ruins and the country's infrastructure collapsed. In 2002 more than 17,000 foreign troops disarmed tens of thousands of rebels and militia fighters, leaving Sierra Leone to face the challenge of reconstruction.

16

1963 THE SOVIETS LAUNCH THE FIRST WOMAN INTO SPACE.
A former textile worker from the Soviet Union became the first woman in space. Lieutenant Valentina Tereshkova was the fifth Russian cosmonaut and the first woman to go into the Earth's orbit when her spaceship *Vostok VI* was launched. Thousands of jubilant women gathered in Red Square, Moscow, to celebrate the occasion. Tereshkova and her fellow cosmonaut Colonel Bykovsky landed safely by parachute two days later in Kazakhstan. Tereshkova had completed 49 orbits of the Earth in two days, 22 hours and 50 minutes. Tereshkova subsequently became active in the Communist Party and never returned to space.

65

1976 Hundreds die in the Soweto race riots between black demonstrators and police in South African townships.

17

1961 RUSSIAN BALLET DANCER RUDOLF NUREYEV DEFECTS TO THE WEST.
Rudolf Nureyev was the principal dancer of the prestigious Kirov Ballet based in Leningrad (now St Petersburg). He broke free from Russian embassy guards at a Paris airport and requested asylum in France. Within a week of his defection, Nureyev was signed up by the Grand Ballet du Marquis de Cuevas in Paris. After meeting leading British dancer Margot Fonteyn, he came to the Royal Ballet in London, which became the base for the rest of his dancing career. Nureyev and Fonteyn's legendary first performance together was at the Royal Opera House, Covent Garden, in the ballet *Giselle* on 21 February 1962.

Nureyev, regarded as one of the greatest male dancers of the twentieth century, never returned to Russia. He died on 6 January 1993.

18

1979 WORLD LEADERS SIGN SALT II TREATY TO LIMIT WEAPONS.

In Vienna, Austria, US president Jimmy Carter and Soviet leader Leonid Brezhnev signed the SALT (Strategic Arms Limitation Talks) II treaty. By doing so, the two world superpowers agreed to limit the number of missile launchers to 2,400 for each side. Negotiations for the deal followed Salt I, which had been signed by US president Richard Nixon and Brezhnev in 1972. This froze the deployment of land-based intercontinental ballistic missiles and banned the construction of any new submarine-based missiles.

While Salt II dealt mainly with the limitation of nuclear weapon launchers, President Carter also outlined plans for wide-ranging arms reduction negotiations over the next decade. Although the Salt II treaty ran into difficulties with the US Senate, on 3 January 1980 President Carter himself asked the Senate to delay its consideration following the Soviet invasion of Afghanistan.

The treaty remained unratified, but President Carter did make a statement saying the USA would comply with its intentions so long as the Soviet Union did the same.

1942 Sir Paul McCartney, member of the famous 1960s British rock band the Beatles, is born in Liverpool, England.

19

1978 CRICKETER IAN BOTHAM BECOMES THE FIRST MAN TO SCORE A CENTURY AND TAKE EIGHT WICKETS IN ONE INNINGS OF A TEST MATCH.

The Somerset all-rounder's performance helped England to victory against Pakistan in the second Cornhill Test, and put Ian Botham in the record books. He hit 108 runs in England's first innings and then took eight wickets for just 34 runs in Pakistan's second innings.

In a career that lasted from 1977 to 1992, Botham was a Test team captain and played in 102 Test matches. His highest-ever batting score was 208 and his best bowling performance was eight wickets for 34 runs. When he retired he became a television commentator and has been a prominent charity fundraiser, undertaking long-distance walks to raise money for Leukaemia Research. He became the charity's first president in 2003.

Ian Botham was appointed an Officer of the Order of the British Empire (OBE) in 1992 for his services to cricket and charity, and received a knighthood in 2007.

20

1976 WESTERNERS EVACUATED FROM BEIRUT.

Nearly 300 westerners, mostly Americans and Britons, were moved from Beirut and taken to safety in Syria by the US military. A US Navy ship rescued about 270 people, including 97 Britons, from the war-torn Lebanese city after attempts to move them by road were ruled out as too dangerous. Most of the refugees were Americans responding to their government's call to leave Beirut following the murder of the US ambassador, Francis Meloy.

From 1975 until the early 1990s, Lebanon suffered a bloody civil war in which regional powers – particularly Israel, Syria and the Palestine Liberation Organisation - used the country as a battlefield for their own conflicts.

1960 Mali and Senegal are declared independent of France.

21

1982 PRINCE WILLIAM IS BORN.

Prince William is second in the line of succession to the British throne after his father, the Prince of Wales. The eldest son of Prince Charles and the late Diana, Princess of Wales, William Arthur Philip Louis was born at St Mary's Hospital in London. William's brother, Prince Harry, was born on 15 September 1984. Aged 13, William went to Eton and then completed a Geography degree at St Andrew's University in Scotland. In 2006 the prince joined the army, entering the officer training academy at Sandhurst and is currently serving in the Blues and Royals regiment of the British Army's Household Cavalry.

Prince William's parents divorced in 1996, and his mother was killed in a car accident in Paris on 31 August 1997. On 1 July 2007, Prince William and Prince Harry organised the 'Concert for Diana' to celebrate their mother's life and charitable work.

67

22

1941 GERMAN FORCES INVADE THE SOVIET UNION IN THE SECOND WORLD WAR.

German troops pushed into the Soviet Union from the south and west, with a third force making its way from the north towards Leningrad (now known as St Petersburg). The invasion, known as Operation Barbarossa, broke the non-aggression pact signed by Germany and the Soviet Union in 1939.

Over the next six months Germany occupied what is now Belarus and most of Ukraine, and surrounded Leningrad. However, the German Army met a courageous resistance from the Soviet Red Army. Retreating troops destroyed crops and burnt entire villages under Soviet leader Joseph Stalin's 'scorched-earth' policy, which aimed to prevent supplies falling into German hands.

The German Army was finally driven back by a surprise counter-attack by the Red Army on 6 December 1941. In 1943 the German 6th Army surrendered at the Battle of Stalingrad. The siege of Leningrad to the north also ended in German defeat in 1944. After 900 days of fighting Hitler faced his first major defeat on land in a significant setback for Nazi Germany.

23

1992 MAFIA BOSS JOHN GOTTI IS SENTENCED TO LIFE IN PRISON.
New York Mafia gangster John Gotti was sentenced to life in prison after being found guilty on 14 counts of conspiracy to commit murder and racketeering.

Gotti, known as the 'Teflon Don' because charges against him never stuck, was born in 1940, the fifth of 13 children, and grew up on the 'mean streets' of New York City. As a teenager he was leader of a local gang and later became involved with the Gambino family, which controlled one of New York's largest organised-crime syndicates. Gotti quickly rose through the ranks of the underworld; with his violent, outspoken personality and flamboyant style, he soon became New York's best-known organised-crime leader.

Despite widespread publicity of his criminal activities, he managed to avoid conviction several times, usually through witness intimidation. However, when one of his accomplices agreed to testify against him, Gotti was found guilty and imprisoned for life without parole. He died in prison in 2002.

1972 The French footballer Zinedine Zidane is born.

24

1932 THE KING OF THAILAND IS OVERTHROWN.
The Promoters Revolution, also known as the Revolution of 1932, put an end to absolute monarchy in Thailand, and heralded the 'Constitutional Era'. On 24 June 1932, the Thai king, Prajadhipok, was ousted in a coup led by a group of men often referred to as the 'promoters'. They included members of the Thai elite, noted intellectuals and some European-educated and disaffected army officers.

The traditional pattern of life in Thailand had altered drastically under the impact of Western ideas, and opposition to the institution of monarchy had grown. The revolution brought about first a temporary constitution, which stripped the king of his powers and which was essentially a dictatorship run by a small group of promoters, calling itself the People's Party. The permanent constitution that followed restored some nominal powers to the Crown.

25

1950 THE UNITED NATIONS CONDEMN NORTH KOREA'S INVASION OF SOUTH KOREA.
Korea had been occupied by Japan from 1910, but following Japan's defeat in the Second World War, the country was split. The Soviet Union accepted the surrender north of the 38th parallel and the United States accepted the surrender to the south of it. This led to a political division between communist North Korea and republican South Korea.

On 24 June 1950, North Korea invaded South Korea at several points along the two countries' joint border. The republican government fled to the South Korean capital, Seoul, and on 25 June America offered military aid to South Korea to counter what it saw as Russian-backed communist aggression. On 28 June North Korean troops entered the capital and took control. The United Nations invoked military sanctions shortly afterwards.

The Korean War cost millions of military and civilian lives, and fighting did not stop until 1953 with the signing of the armistice on 27 July. A peace deal has never been reached and reunification never achieved. US troops remain in the demilitarised zone on and around the 38th parallel separating North and South Korea.

26

1963 US PRESIDENT JOHN F. KENNEDY'S 'ICH BIN EIN BERLINER' SPEECH MARKS A TURNING-POINT IN THE COLD WAR.

After the end of the Second World War, Nazi Germany and its capital Berlin were divided into four zones occupied and controlled by the Allied powers. The advent of the Cold War – the period of conflict and competition between the United States and the Soviet Union – caused the French, British and American zones to be formed into the Federal Republic of Germany (including West Berlin) in 1949. The Soviet zone then formed the German Democratic Republic (including East Berlin) the same year. In 1961, the Berlin Wall was constructed to divide East and West Berlin. It remained in place for 28 years.

The US president's groundbreaking speech in Berlin in 1963 offered American solidarity to the citizens of West Germany. Two months later, President Kennedy negotiated the first Nuclear Test Ban Treaty with the Soviet Union, in what was seen as a first step towards ending the Cold War. The Berlin Wall was finally brought down in November 1989 and Germany was reunited in October 1990.

69

27

1991 YUGOSLAV TROOPS SEIZE CONTROL IN SLOVENIA, 48 HOURS AFTER IT DECLARES INDEPENDENCE.

Yugoslav tanks, troops and aircraft swept into the small republic of Slovenia and federal forces moved to seize control of border crossing points with Italy, Austria and Hungary. More government tanks rolled into neighbouring Croatia, which was also seeking independence.

Marshall Tito, who formed communist Yugoslavia in 1945, had created a federation of six republics: Croatia, Montenegro, Serbia, Slovenia, Bosnia-Herzegovina, Macedonia. But ethnic tensions continued in the volatile Balkan states, and in 1980, the federation fell apart rapidly after Slovenia's declaration of independence. A bitter conflict developed, characterised by huge numbers of refugees, ethnic hatred and atrocities committed by all sides. An uneasy peace was achieved in December 1995 with the Dayton Accord.

28

2004 THE US TRANSFERS POWER BACK TO IRAQ.

The US handed power back to the Iraqi people at a ceremony in Baghdad, ending 15 months of US control in the war-torn country. On 20 March 2003 the US-led invasion of Iraq took place when US president George W. Bush and British prime minister Tony Blair argued that Iraq's development of weapons of mass destruction posed a threat to the US, its allies and interests.

The European Union and NATO alliance both pledged their support for Iyad Allawi's interim government. The first multi-party elections in 50 years took place in January 2005 and an interim, democratically elected government was sworn in with Shia Ibrahim Jaafari as prime minister. Iraqi leader Saddam Hussein was tried by the interim Iraqi government for 'crimes against humanity'. He was hanged on 30 December 2006. American and British troops have remained in Iraq and have not yet committed to a date when they will withdraw. Frequent attacks by insurgent troops continue.

29

1995 US SPACE SHUTTLE *ATLANTIS* DOCKS WITH THE RUSSIAN MIR SPACE STATION.

American and Russian spacecraft successfully docked in orbit for the first time in 20 years, signalling a new era of space cooperation between the two former Cold War rivals. The operation to link the craft was led by the commander of the *Atlantis*, Robert Gibson. After the pressure between the two crafts was equalised, Gibson opened the hatch separating them and propelled himself through to the Russian craft to shake hands with his Russian counterpart. The crew of the US shuttle then moved into the Mir space station.

After 15 years in space, the Mir space station returned to Earth in March 2001. It had circled the Earth about 88,000 times, travelling 3.6 billion km (2.2 billion miles).

1986 Richard Branson holds the new world record for the fastest crossing of the Atlantic in the *Virgin Atlantic Challenger*.

30

1992 FORMER BRITISH PRIME MINISTER MARGARET THATCHER TAKES HER PLACE IN THE HOUSE OF LORDS.

Former prime minister Margaret Thatcher took her place in the House of Lords as Baroness Thatcher of Kesteven. Thatcher was elected MP for Finchley in 1959 and succeeded Edward Heath as leader of the Conservative Party in 1975. She became Britain's first woman prime minister in 1979, and was the longest-serving prime minister of the twentieth century. She was replaced as Tory leader by John Major in 1990.

July

1

1997 THE BRITISH HAND HONG KONG OVER TO THE CHINESE.
Britain had controlled Hong Kong since 1842, apart from a brief period during the Second World War when the Japanese took over. Discussions between Britain and China on the future of Hong Kong began in 1982 and British prime minister Margaret Thatcher and her Chinese counterpart, Zhao Ziyang, signed the Joint Declaration in 1984.

Hong Kong was given back at a handover ceremony at the Convention Centre. Prince Charles, British prime minister Tony Blair, foreign secretary Robin Cook, Hong Kong governor Chris Patten and Chinese dignitaries including the president Jiang Zemin, premier Li Peng, foreign minister Qian Qichen and General Zhang Wannian attended the ceremony. Tung Chee-hwa was sworn in as Hong Kong's new leader.

1994 The Chairman of the Palestinian Liberation Organisation (PLO), Yasser Arafat, returns to the Gaza strip after 27 years in exile.

2

1964 THE CIVIL RIGHTS BILL IS SIGNED IN THE UNITED STATES.
The Civil Rights Bill, regarded as one of the most important pieces of legislation in American history, was signed by US president Lyndon B. Johnson. It created equal rights in voting, education, public accommodations and union membership, regardless of race, colour, religion or national origin. After the signing, President Johnson shook hands with civil rights leader Dr Martin Luther King Jr.

The bill had caused much controversy since it was introduced the previous year by John F. Kennedy, and the rest of the decade witnessed race riots and assassinations, with the shooting of Malcolm X in 1965 and of Martin Luther King Jr in 1968.

2005 Music stars perform at Live 8 concerts around the world to draw attention to global poverty.

3

1987 NAZI WAR CRIMINAL KLAUS BARBIE IS SENTENCED TO LIFE IMPRISONMENT.
Klaus Barbie, the former Gestapo chief in Lyon from 1942 to 1944, was sentenced to life imprisonment for crimes against humanity. Known as the Butcher of Lyon, Barbie was found guilty of charges of deporting people to concentration camps in

Germany during the Second World War. In one deportation, 44 children were rounded up in a farmhouse at Izieu and sent to their deaths. Barbie is blamed for 4,000 deaths and a further 7,500 deportations during the war. He died in prison in Lyon on 25 September 1991.

4

1995 JOHN MAJOR WINS THE CONSERVATIVE LEADERSHIP CONTEST.
John Major took over as leader of the party when Margaret Thatcher was ousted by the Conservatives in 1990. He inherited a party split on the issue of European Union and his resignation as leader in June 1995 was widely seen as an attempt to bring to a head divisions in the party over European policy. His sole challenger in the ensuing leadership contest was Welsh secretary John Redwood. Major received backing from 218 of the party's MPs in the leadership ballot, against 89 votes for Redwood. Major resigned as Conservative Party leader two years later, following Labour's victory in the 1997 general election. He was succeeded by William Hague.

5

1975 AMERICAN TENNIS PLAYER ARTHUR ASHE BECOMES THE FIRST BLACK MAN TO WIN WIMBLEDON.
Arthur Ashe became the first black man to win the Wimbledon singles championship against defending champion Jimmy Connors. Later in 1975, Ashe was ranked No. 1 tennis seed in the world. He suffered a heart attack in 1979 and retired as a professional player in 1980. Throughout his life Ashe used his sporting profile to campaign on a variety of political issues. He protested against apartheid in South Africa and US treatment of refugees arriving in the country from Haiti. He died in 1993.

6

1997 NASA SPACE BUGGY STARTS EXPLORING MARS.
NASA scientists freed a roving space probe from the Mars Pathfinder to begin its long-awaited exploration of the Red Planet. The rover, known as *Sojourner*, was the first man-made craft to travel over the surface of another planet. It weighed just 10 kg (22 lb), and was about the size of a bread-bin. Pathfinder sent back images of the surface of Mars, showing the tracks made by *Sojourner*'s six studded titanium wheels.

Sojourner continued to explore Mars for nearly three months, covering more than 42,000 sq m (450,000 sq ft) and sending back 550 images of the Martian surface. It was controlled remotely from California, USA. Exploration on Mars continued and in 2001, the Mars Odyssey provided a remarkable geological map of the planet and in 2004, NASA's Mars rovers, *Spirit* and *Opportunity*, discovered compelling evidence for the prolonged presence of water on the planet's surface.

2005 The International Olympic Committee announces that London is to host the 2012 Olympic Games.

7

2005 AL-QAEDA BOMB ATTACKS ON LONDON KILL 52 AND INJURE 700.
Attacks on London's transport network were carried out by four suicide bombers.
There were three explosions on the Underground at Liverpool Street, Edgware Road
and between King's Cross and Russell Square. There was also a blast on a double-
decker bus at Tavistock Square. British prime minister Tony Blair flew back from the
G8 World Poverty Summit in Gleneagles, Scotland to condemn the terrorists and
pledge to continue to wage war on terrorism.

Al-Qaeda, an international Islamic terrorist organisation attacking non-Islamic
governments with force and violence, issued a video-taped statement in September
claiming it was behind the London bombings. On 9 July 2007 four men, Muktar Said
Ibrahim, Yassin Omar, Hussain Osman and Ramzi Mohammed were tried and found
guilty of conspiracy to murder in a further plot to bomb London on 21 July 2005.
They were sentenced to life imprisonment with a recommendation that they should
serve a minimum of 40 years.

8

2000 J. K. ROWLING'S BOOK *HARRY POTTER AND THE GOBLET OF FIRE*
BREAKS ALL PUBLISHING RECORDS.
The fourth instalment in J. K. Rowling's *Harry Potter* series of fantasy novels was
released simultaneously on both sides of the Atlantic, with an initial print-run of 5.3
million, with 1.5 million in Britain and 3.8 million in the United States. By the time
of its release, the previous three books: *Harry Potter and the Philosopher's Stone*,
Harry Potter and the Chamber of Secrets and *Harry Potter and the Prisoner of
Azkaban*, had achieved worldwide sales of 35 million copies in 31 languages.

When *Harry Potter and the Order of the Phoenix* was published in 2003, five
million copies were sold within 24 hours of its release. The sixth title, *Harry Potter
and the Half-Blood Prince*, was published in 2005 and the final book in the series,
Harry Potter and the Deathly Hallows hit the shelves on 21 July 2007, marking the
final chapter of a publishing phenomenon. Rowling dreamt up Harry Potter in 1990.
The success of the novels has made her the highest-earning novelist in literary history.
The first five novels have been made into films, starring Daniel Radcliffe as Harry
Potter. They have all been major box office successes.

9

1940 THE LUFTWAFFE LAUNCHES THE BATTLE OF BRITAIN.
The German Air Force, the Luftwaffe, launched its first major assault on Britain with
a series of attacks on shipping convoys off the south-east coast of England. On 16
July 1940 Hitler had ordered preparations for Operation Sealion, the codename for
the invasion of Britain. Given Britain's naval superiority, Hitler knew that an invasion
would be made easier if Germany could establish control of the air in the battle zone.
The ensuing battle for control of the skies became known as the Battle of Britain.

The Luftwaffe had 750 long-range and 250 dive bombers, 600 single-engined and 150 twin-engined fighters, which was significantly more than RAF Fighter Command's 600 planes. But the British forces were better prepared, with radar technology giving advance warning of the German bombing raids. The air attacks gradually moved inland, and in August, Germany targeted London. Britain retaliated by bombing the German capital, Berlin.

German forces later switched to night-time air raids, which continued until March 1941, when Britain finally won the Battle of Britain.

1947 An extraterrestrial spacecraft is rumoured to have crash-landed at Roswell in New Mexico, USA.

10

1987 SOLDIERS REMEMBER THE FIRST WORLD WAR BATTLE OF PASSCHENDAELE.
Seventy years on, veteran soldiers returned to the scene of the bloodiest battle of the First World War. The fields of Passchendaele in Belgium claimed the lives of 250,000 troops of the British Commonwealth between July and November 1917. The British Army had expected to reach Passchendaele in two days, before advancing to drive the Germans behind the Rhine as part of the Big Push to end the war. But it took the Allied troops 99 days to capture the decimated village of Passchendaele in south-west Flanders. There were nearly half a million losses on both sides. The British gained just 8 km (5 miles) at a cost of around 35 lives per metre.

The First World War finally ended in November 1918. A total of 65 million soldiers had been involved in the battle. Of these, 21 million were wounded and 10 million were killed. The British Empire lost a total of 950,000 servicemen, while France, Germany and the Russian Empire each lost well over a million. For many the Battle of Passchendaele symbolised the futility of war and the needless slaughter of human life.

11

1914 BABE RUTH PLAYS HIS FIRST MAJOR LEAGUE BASEBALL GAME.
The professional baseball player George Herman Ruth, nicknamed 'Babe', escaped a life of poverty to become one of America's most celebrated athletes. On 11 July 1914, he played in his first major league baseball game, for the Boston Red Sox. Ruth soon became the best left-handed pitcher in baseball. Between 1915 and 1919 he won 85 games, yielded a stunning earned run average of only 2.02 and won three World Series games (one in 1916 and two in 1918).

In 1920 he was sold to the New York Yankees and, as a full-time outfielder, emerged as the greatest hitter to have ever played the game.

1921 Mongolia declares independence from China.

12

1990 RUSSIAN PRESIDENT BORIS YELTSIN RESIGNS FROM THE SOVIET COMMUNIST PARTY.
When Boris Yeltsin, president of the Russian parliament, resigned from the Soviet Communist Party it split the Soviet communists, with the influential radical reform group Democratic Platform also breaking away. The split left Soviet leader Mikhail Gorbachev with a divided party for the first time since the Bolshevik-Menshevik divide that had put Lenin in power in 1903. In the following days, thousands of demonstrators gathered beside the walls of the Kremlin to voice their opposition to the Soviet Communist Party.

In August 1991, the battle between reformists and conservatives resulted in an attempted coup against Gorbachev. Yeltsin became a national hero after he mounted a tank to rally the people against the coup. After the formal collapse of the Soviet Union later in 1991, Boris Yeltsin, who was already president of Russia, became the head of a world superpower.

Yeltsin stood down from the presidency on 1 January 2000. His chosen successor, Vladimir Putin, won the next election a few months later.

13

1985 LIVE AID RAISES £40 MILLION FOR FAMINE RELIEF IN AFRICA.
The world's biggest rock festival was organised by Boomtown Rats singer Bob Geldof to raise money for famine relief in Africa. Television pictures of the star-studded event were transmitted to more than 1.5 billion people in 160 countries. The concert started with Status Quo performing 'Rockin' All Over the World'.

Nine months earlier the droughts, disease and famine in north-eastern Africa were brought to the world's attention. After seeing BBC news reports Bob Geldof and Midge Ure, the singer from Ultravox, wrote the song 'Do They Know It's Christmas?' to raise money for the crisis. Performing under the name Band Aid, they released the song with vocals by a host of stars, including Bono and George Michael, on 7 December 1984. It raised £8 million. Geldof was given an honorary knighthood in 1986. On 2 July 2005 he organised Live 8, a series of rock concerts around the world to raise awareness about global poverty.

1955 Ruth Ellis is the last woman hanged in Britain, for the murder of David Blakely. The death penalty in Britain was finally removed in 1970.

14

1938 FILM DIRECTOR ALFRED HITCHCOCK SIGNS WITH DAVID O. SELZNICK.
The son of a London poultry dealer and fruit importer, Alfred Hitchcock entered show business when he was hired to design silent-film title cards. In that capacity, he

worked closely with screenwriters, who occasionally allowed him to direct minor scenes. He became a director in 1925.

On 14 July 1938 Hitchcock signed a contract with film producer David O. Selznick to direct movies in Hollywood. Hitchcock had already established a reputation as England's foremost director with such films as *The Thirty-Nine Steps*, *The Man Who Knew Too Much* and *The Lady Vanishes*. Alfred Hitchcock's first American film, *Rebecca*, starring Laurence Olivier and Joan Fontaine, opened in 1940 and won Academy Awards for Best Picture and Best Cinematography. Over the next 30 years he continued to make films within the Hollywood studio system, among them suspenseful thrillers such as *Psycho* (1960), *The Birds* (1963) and *Marnie* (1964).

1995 The MP3 technical format is named.

15

1965 CLOSE-UP PICTURES OF MARS ARE PROVIDED BY *MARINER 4*.
Mariner 4, an unmanned space probe launched by NASA in 1964, flew by Mars and returned close-up pictures of its surface. Since the end of the nineteenth century some people had suspected that systems of long, straight surface lines seen on Mars might be canals created by intelligent alien beings. The pictures beamed back on 15 July 1965 proved that the planet's rumoured canals were actually illusions.

1997 Italian fashion designer Gianni Versace is shot dead on the steps of his mansion in Miami, USA.

16

1945 ALLIED LEADERS GATHER AT POTSDAM TO DECIDE THE FUTURE OF DEFEATED GERMANY.
British prime minister Winston Churchill, US president Harry S. Truman and leader of the Soviet Union, Joseph Stalin gathered in the German city of Potsdam to review the political and economic situation in Europe following the surrender of Germany at the end of the Second World War. Their aim was to strip Germany of its military and economic power to prevent any future attempts to expand. As a result of Potsdam, the Nazi Party was outlawed and Germany and its capital Berlin were divided into four zones, each one occupied by an allied nation (Britain, the USA, the USSR and France).

On 26 July the leaders issued a statement known as the Potsdam Declaration, demanding Japan's unconditional surrender by 28 July. When Japan refused the terms of the agreement, the United States dropped the atomic bomb on Hiroshima on 6 August and on Nagasaki on 9 August. This was also the day that Soviet forces invaded Japanese-occupied Manchuria in China. Japan officially surrendered on 2 September 1945, marking the end of the Second World War.

1955 Stirling Moss is the first Englishman to win the British Grand Prix.

17

1936 START OF THE SPANISH CIVIL WAR.
The uprising that was to escalate into the Spanish Civil War began in garrison towns throughout Spain. Conservative nationalist rebels seized control of Spanish Morocco, the Canary Islands and the Balearic Islands (except Minorca). They also gained control of the part of Spain north of the Guadarrama mountains and the Ebro River, except for Asturias, Santander and the Basque provinces along the north coast and the region of Catalonia in the north-east. The republican government responded by putting down nationalist uprisings. Soon events spiralled into a bloody catalogue of violence and retribution that lasted until 1939, when the nationalists and Francisco Franco assumed power.

1918 Tsar Nicholas II of Russia and his family are assassinated.

18

1925 VOLUME I OF ADOLF HITLER'S *MEIN KAMPF* IS PUBLISHED.
Hitler wrote the first volume of *Mein Kampf*, the political manifesto that became the bible of Nazism in Germany's Third Reich, from his prison cell in Bavaria. Entitled *Die Abrechnung* ('The Settlement [of Accounts]', or 'Revenge'), it was published on 18 July 1925. Two years later the second volume was published. By 1939, *Mein Kampf* had sold 5,200,000 copies and had been translated into 11 languages.

The first volume examines the world of Hitler's youth, the First World War, and the 'betrayal' of Germany's collapse in 1918. It also expresses Hitler's racist ideology, identifying the Aryan as the 'genius' race and the Jew as the 'parasite'. It was necessary, Hitler wrote, for Germans to 'occupy themselves not merely with the breeding of dogs, horses, and cats but also with care for the purity of their own blood'. It was such beliefs that led to Hitler's 'Final Solution' and the establishment of the labour and death camps during the Second World War.

1918 South African black nationalist leader and statesman Nelson Mandela is born.

19

1983 THE SKELETON OF FLESH-EATING DINOSAUR GOES ON VIEW AT THE NATURAL HISTORY MUSEUM IN LONDON.
Amateur fossil hunter Bill Walker had found a foot-long claw belonging to a flesh-eating dinosaur at a clay pit in Surrey in January. Palaeontologists dated the remains at 125 million years old, or from the Cretaceous period. It was a totally new species of fish-eating dinosaur and would have weighed half as much as an elephant, with a skull and teeth similar to a crocodile. It was subsequently named *Baryonyx Walkeri*, meaning 'Mr Walker's heavy claw'.

20

1974 TURKEY INVADES CYPRUS.

Tension had been running high in the Mediterranean island of Cyprus since a military coup five days earlier that had deposed Greek Cypriot president Archbishop Makarios. Makarios became the republic's first elected president in 1959 after agreeing to give up plans for a union with Greece. The coup led to fears among the Turkish Cypriot community that there would be an attempt to unify Cyprus with Greece.

A ceasefire was signed on 22 July and the foreign ministers of Greece, Turkey and Britain – as former colonial ruler of Cyprus – began talks on a new constitution on 25 July. But talks to settle the crisis diplomatically failed. In February 1975, the Turks announced the establishment of the Turkish Federated State of Cyprus, with Turkish Cypriot leader Rauf Denktash becoming president. Eight years later they declared themselves an independent state, recognised only by Turkey. In 2004 a referendum was held on a United Nations' plan to reunite the island. It gained support from the Turkish side, but was rejected by the Greeks.

1960 Sirimavo Bandaranaike becomes leader of Ceylon (since renamed Sri Lanka) and the world's first-ever female prime minister.

21

1969 AMERICAN ASTRONAUT NEIL ARMSTRONG BECOMES THE FIRST MAN TO WALK ON THE MOON.

The American Moon landing marked the pinnacle of the space race between the USA and USSR. As Neil Armstrong stepped on to the Moon's surface he declared: 'That's one small step for man, one giant leap for mankind.'

The historic events were captured on television cameras installed on the spacecraft *Eagle*. Armstrong spent his first few minutes on the Moon taking photographs and soil samples. When he was joined by colleague Edwin 'Buzz' Aldrin, the two astronauts planted the US flag on the Moon's surface. They also unveiled a plaque bearing President Nixon's signature and an inscription, reading:

'*Here men from the planet Earth first set foot upon the Moon July 1969 AD. We came in peace for all mankind.*'

1994 Tony Blair, MP for Sedgefield, is confirmed as the new leader of the Labour Party in Britain.

22

1977 DISGRACED DEPUTY PRIME MINISTER OF CHINA, DENG XIAOPING, RETURNS TO THE CHINESE GOVERNMENT.

The Chinese Communist Party (CCP) conference restored Deng Xiaoping to the offices of vice-premier of the state council, vice-chairman of the central committee, vice-chairman of the military commission and chief of the general staff of the People's

Liberation Army. He had been dismissed after the left-wing Gang of Four blamed him for the popular uprising in Tiananmen Square in April 1976 after Premier Zhou Enlai's death. Since the death of Chairman Mao in September 1976, the Gang of Four had attempted a programme of radical reform. The gang's members were formally expelled from the CCP, arrested and put on trial in 1980 for their part in an attempted coup.

By the end of 1978 Deng Xiaoping had taken over from Premier Hua Guofeng. In 1978 he oversaw the historic change of direction for China involving the so-called 'Four Modernisations' of agriculture, industry, national defence, and science and technology. He resigned from his last official party post in 1989, after he was one of the party members who ordered the use of military force to clear the Tiananmen Square protests in 1989. He died on 19 February 1997.

23

1995 BRITISH FORCES ARE SENT TO THE BESIEGED BOSNIAN CAPITAL OF SARAJEVO.

Sarajevo was one of six UN-designated 'safe havens' in war-torn Bosnia, set up to protect Muslim communities during the Bosnian conflict. By July 1995 Serbian forces were attacking all six areas, including Zepa and Srebrenica, which were lost to Serbian control amidst large-scale death and human-rights atrocities. The UN finally agreed to launch NATO air strikes against the Bosnian Serbs at the end of August after a Serbian mortar killed 38 people in Sarajevo.

In December 1995 the Muslim, Serb and Croat warring factions returned to the negotiating table and eventually brought an end to the Bosnian conflict at Dayton, Ohio.

24

1917 MATA HARI'S TRIAL BEGINS IN FRANCE

The Dutch-born dancer and courtesan Mata Hari went on trial, accused of spying for Germany during the First World War. Born Margaretha Geertruida Zelle in 1876, Mata Hari spent some time in Java and Sumatra with her husband, an army officer. It is there that she learnt various 'exotic' dances and where she found the inspiration for her stage name.

On her return to Europe, Margaretha separated from her husband and found work as a professional dancer in Paris, calling herself Mata Hari, a Malay expression for the Sun. Her statuesque height, beauty and willingness to appear virtually nude in the theatre made her a huge success in Paris and other major European cities.

It is not clear whether or not Mata Hari was actually a spy, but according to one account, in 1916 while she was living in The Hague, a German consul is said to have offered to pay her for whatever information she could obtain on her next trip to France. On her arrest in Paris, she claimed that she had only given some outdated information to a German intelligence officer. However, French suspicion of her increased and she was imprisoned, tried by a military court on 24 and 25 July 1917, sentenced to death, and shot by a firing squad.

25

1978 THE WORLD'S FIRST 'TEST-TUBE BABY' IS BORN.
Louise Brown was born in Manchester, UK, after her mother underwent in vitro fertility (IVF) treatment. An embryo of the mother's egg and the father's sperm was implanted in the mother's womb after it had been fertilised in a laboratory. The technique had been pioneered by Patrick Steptoe and Robert Edwards. By the time Louise Brown celebrated her twenty-first birthday in 1999, 300,000 women worldwide had conceived through IVF.

26

1956 EGYPT SEIZES CONTROL OF THE SUEZ CANAL.
The Suez Canal runs from Port Said on the Mediterranean to Suez on the Red Sea, and is an important waterway for world trade and a major source of revenue for Britain. Egypt's president, Colonel Gamal Abdel Nasser, announced the nationalisation of the Suez Canal Company to provide funding for the construction of the Aswan Dam. The move came after the withdrawal of British and American funding towards the new dam.

Nasser also blockaded Israel's only outlet to the Red Sea, the Straits of Tiran. Britain and France joined forces with Israel, an alliance that was denied for many years, and on 29 October 1956, Israeli troops invaded Egypt's Sinai Peninsula. Two days later, the British and French invaded Egypt's canal zone after Nasser had refused to allow the creation of a buffer zone between Israel and Egypt. When the Soviet Union threatened to intervene on Egypt's behalf, US president Dwight D. Eisenhower feared that the USSR were using the crisis as a way of gaining power in the Middle East. He pressured Britain, France and Israel into agreeing to a ceasefire and eventual withdrawal from Egypt in November 1956.

1945 Labour's Clement Attlee is elected Britain's new prime minister, defeating Britain's war-time coalition leader, Winston Churchill.

27

1996 BOMB EXPLODES AT ATLANTA OLYMPICS IN GEORGIA, USA.
A bomb exploded at a crowded concert in Atlanta, Georgia, the city hosting the 1996 Olympic Games. Two people were killed and 200 were injured. On 29 January 1998, an abortion clinic was bombed in Birmingham, Alabama, killing an off-duty police officer and critically wounding a nurse. A car reported at the crime scene was later found abandoned. Investigators traced it to Eric Robert Rudolph, a 31-year-old carpenter. Although Rudolph was not immediately found, authorities positively identified him as the culprit in the Birmingham and Atlanta bombings, and an extensive manhunt began. He was finally captured on 31 May 2003.

1949 The world's first jet-propelled airliner, the Comet, designed by British aircraft pioneer Geoffrey de Havilland, makes its test flight in England.

28

1988 PADDY ASHDOWN BECOMES THE FIRST LEADER OF THE NEW SOCIAL AND LIBERAL DEMOCRAT PARTY.
Paddy Ashdown, the MP for Yeoville, won a decisive victory with nearly 72 per cent of the votes against former deputy leader of the Liberal Party, Alan Beith, to lead Britain's third political party. Ashdown led the SLD, later the Liberal Democrats, until 1999. He was succeeded as party leader by Charles Kennedy. Ashdown retired from the House of Commons just before the 2001 general election, and Labour prime minister Tony Blair made him a peer in the same year. An ex-Royal Marines officer, he became the international community's high representative in Bosnia-Herzegovina in 2002.

1976 An estimated half a million people die in the Tangshan earthquake in China.

29

1981 PRINCE CHARLES AND LADY DIANA SPENCER MARRY.
Prince Charles and Lady Diana Spencer were married at St Paul's Cathedral before an invited congregation of 3,500 and an estimated global television audience of 750 million. Crowds of 600,000 people filled the streets of London to watch the wedding procession and there was a national holiday in Britain to mark the occasion.

81

The couple's first son, Prince William, was born on 21 June 1982, and their second, Prince Harry, on 15 September 1984. Charles and Diana separated in 1993 and divorced in 1996. Diana was killed in a car crash in Paris in 1997. Prince Charles married Camilla Parker Bowles on 9 April 2005.

30

1966 ENGLAND WINS FOOTBALL'S WORLD CUP FOR THE FIRST TIME.
A crowd of 93,000 spectators at London's Wembley Stadium watched England play West Germany in the final game of the 1966 championships. Another 400 million people around the world watched the match on television. Bobby Moore captained the England squad. In the final moments of extra time Geoff Hurst scored his third goal to give England a 4-2 victory. Hurst became the first man ever to score a hat-trick in a World Cup final but his second goal was controversial, and only given after consultation between the Swiss referee and Soviet linesman.

England have failed to reach the World Cup final since 1966. Germany went on to compete in five more finals and have won the championships three times, against Hungary in 1954, Holland in 1974 and Argentina in 1990.

31

1991 THE STRATEGIC ARMS REDUCTION TREATY IS SIGNED.
The historic Strategic Arms Reduction Treaty, known as Start, reduced the stockpiles of nuclear warheads of the United States and Soviet Union by about 35 per cent. The agreement was signed by US president George Bush and Soviet leader Mikhail Gorbachev. The agreement took more than nine years to negotiate and reduced each nation's strategic nuclear weapons over seven years. The Soviet Union collapsed in December 1991, before the Start treaty could be ratified. Agreements were eventually reached with the Russian Federation and the Ukraine, Belarus and Kazakhstan, the three former Soviet states where nuclear weapons were stationed.

The Start treaty finally came into effect in December 1994 and the targets set out in the treaty were eventually met in 2001. In 1993, the Start II treaty agreed to scrap a further 3,000-3,500 warheads. Eventually Start II and its successor Start III, were superseded by the Strategic Offensive Reductions Treaty. Better known as the Treaty of Moscow, it aims to cut each side's nuclear warheads by approximately 70 per cent.

1998 The UK imposes a total ban on the use of landmines.

August

1

1944 THE POLISH HOME ARMY BEGINS THE BATTLE AGAINST THE GERMANS TO LIBERATE WARSAW.
Warsaw was the first European capital to be captured by the Germans at the start of the Second World War in 1939. The German frontline had already been forced to retreat from a sustained attack by the Russian Red Army, which had forced them out of the Baltic states, Belorussia and western Poland. During the first day's fighting to liberate Warsaw, significant gains were made by the Polish Home Army, with gas, electricity and water services all being returned to Polish hands. The battle for control of Warsaw lasted 63 days. It ended with the Poles surrendering on 3 October 1944, following the successful German counter-offensive that began on 5 August
   Poland's General Bor received no help from the Soviets, who refused to allow the Allies to use Soviet bases to take off and land. Instead, Allied pilots were forced to fly up from Italy and many planes were lost. An estimated 200,000 Polish civilians died during the conflict.

2

1990 IRAQ INVADES KUWAIT, TRIGGERING THE GULF WAR.
Kuwait is small desert country situated between Iraq and Saudi Arabia, but it has a major strategic and trading advantage in that its shore includes a deep harbour on the Persian Gulf. On 2 August 1990, the army of President Saddam Hussein of Iraq invaded Kuwait. Iraq apparently wanted to acquire Kuwait's large oil reserves, but Hussein also wanted to extend Iraq's power in the region.
   On 3 August the United Nations Security Council called for Iraq to withdraw from Kuwait, and on 6 August the council imposed a worldwide ban on trade with Iraq. Hussein refused to withdraw his troops, however, and the USA and its Western European NATO allies sent troops to Saudia Arabia to deter a possible attack there. The Persian Gulf War began on 16 January 1991 with a massive US-led air offensive against Iraq that continued throughout the war. By the end of February 1991, Iraq had been defeated.

1934 Adolf Hitler becomes Führer ('Leader') of Germany.

3

1916 SIR ROGER CASEMENT IS HANGED IN THE UK.
Sir Roger Casement was a distinguished British civil servant who was executed for treason on 3 August 1916. He became a famous Irish martyr in the revolt against British rule in Ireland.

Although he came from a Northern Ireland Protestant family, Casement's sympathies lay with the Roman Catholic nationalists who were fighting to free Ireland from British rule. In 1913 he helped form the Irish National Volunteers, and sought American aid for that anti-British force. After the start of the First World War, he visited Berlin to seek German help for the Irish independence movement, but he discovered that the German government was unwilling to risk an expedition to Ireland at that time.

Casement subsequently tried and failed to obtain the loan of German Army officers to lead an Irish rising planned for Easter 1916. On 12 April he sailed for Ireland in a German submarine, but was arrested when he landed near Tralee, County Kerry. He was taken to London where, on 29 June, he was convicted of treason and sentenced to death.

1936 Black track-and-field athlete Jesse Owens wins the 100 metres gold medal at the Berlin Olympics (Owens won four gold medals in total).

4

2000 THE QUEEN MOTHER CELEBRATES HER CENTENARY.
Celebrations took place all over the United Kingdom to mark the hundredth birthday of Queen Elizabeth, the Queen Mother – the first member of the royal family to reach her centenary birthday.

Born Elizabeth Bowes-Lyon, she married Albert, Duke of York, the second son of George V, in 1923. They had two children, Princess Elizabeth and Princess Margaret. In 1936, following the abdication of his brother, Edward VIII, Albert became George VI and Elizabeth became queen. George VI died in 1952, and his queen became Queen Elizabeth, the Queen Mother, to avoid confusion with the new monarch, Queen Elizabeth II.

A popular and active member of the royal family, the Queen Mother died on 30 March 2002, aged 101. She was buried alongside her husband, King George VI, in St George's chapel, Windsor.

5

1962 DEATH OF AMERICAN MOVIE ICON, MARILYN MONROE.
Marilyn Monroe was born Norma Jean Mortenson in 1926 in Los Angeles, California, USA. She had a troubled childhood, living with 12 successive sets of foster parents and spending time in an orphanage. Later, her stunningly photogenic qualities led to a career as a photographic model and then as a movie actress. Her onscreen mix of vulnerability and sex appeal transfixed audiences and she rapidly became an international superstar.

However, Monroe's private life was dogged with misery, insecurity and addiction, and she was found dead in her apartment at the age of 36. Her death was believed to have been caused by an overdose of sleeping pills.

1930 US astronaut Neil Armstrong, the first person to set foot on the Moon, is born.

6

1945 THE FIRST ATOMIC BOMB IS DROPPED BY THE UNITED STATES ON THE JAPANESE CITY OF HIROSHIMA.

The Hiroshima bomb, known as 'Little Boy', was dropped from an American B-26 Superfortress. It contained the explosive power of 15,000 tonnes of TNT and devastated an area of 13 sq km (5 sq miles). More than 60 per cent of the buildings in the city were destroyed. Official Japanese figures at the time put the death toll at 118,661 civilians, but later estimates suggested the final toll was about 140,000 of Hiroshima's 350,000 population. Many more suffered the long-term effects of the radiation released by the bomb.

Three days later, the United States launched a second, bigger atomic bomb against the city of Nagasaki. The device, known as 'Fat Man', weighed approximately 4,050 kg (8,929 lb). Nearly 74,000 people were killed and a similar number injured.

The two atomic bombs, along with the Soviet declaration of war against Japan on 8 August 1945, led to the Japanese surrender to the Allied Forces. Victory over Japan, or VJ Day, marked the end of combat in the Second World War and was celebrated by the Allied nations on 15 August 1945.

7

1972 ASIANS ARE EXPELLED FROM UGANDA.

The Ugandan leader Idi Amin set a deadline for the expulsion of all Asians who were not Ugandan citizens to leave the country within 90 days. Amin had come to power the previous year, after overthrowing Uganda's elected leader in a military-backed coup. Asians had been living in Uganda, a former British colony, for more than a century. Resentment had been building up against them within Uganda's black majority, fuelled by their economic growth and prosperity. Eventually around 50,000 Asians were forced to leave Uganda, of which 30,000 escaped to Britain. Many arrived virtually penniless, having been expelled without compensation for businesses and property.

Idi Amin was overthrown in 1979 and lived in exile in Saudi Arabia until his death in 2003.

85

8

1991 BRITISH HOSTAGE JOHN MCCARTHY IS FREED.

Journalist John McCarthy was Britain's longest-held hostage in Lebanon. He was held in captivity for over five years by the militant terrorist group Islamic Jihad. For part of his time in captivity, McCarthy was held with other hostages, including fellow Britons Terry Waite and Brian Keenan, and Americans Terry Anderson and Tom Sutherland. There had been a long campaign to free McCarthy, led by his friend Jill Morrell. The two of them wrote a best-selling book, *Some Other Rainbow*, describing his ordeal.

John McCarthy was appointed a Commander of the British Empire (CBE) in 1992.

9

1999 CHARLES KENNEDY BECOMES THE NEW LEADER OF THE LIBERAL DEMOCRATS IN BRITAIN.

Charles Kennedy succeeded Paddy Ashdown as leader of the Liberal Democrats, the third-largest political party in the UK. Kennedy was a strong supporter of the policy of proportional representation in parliamentary elections, and he moved away from the idea of a pact between the Liberal and Labour parties after the Labour government failed to hold a referendum on electoral reform. The 2001 general election gave the Liberal Democrats an enlarged share of the vote, with 52 MPs in parliament.

Charles Kennedy resigned as party leader in January 2006. He was succeeded by Menzies Campbell.

10

1990 THE *MAGELLAN* SPACECRAFT ARRIVES ON VENUS.

NASA's *Magellan* space probe arrived at the planet Venus after a 15-month journey from Earth. Venus is Earth's nearest neighbour, and similar in size, mass and distance from the Sun. But the atmosphere on Venus is almost entirely made up of carbon dioxide and temperatures on its surface are hot enough to melt lead.

Magellan spent four years mapping the planet, producing a detailed radar map of 99 per cent of it. It found evidence of volcanic activity over about 85 per cent of its surface. In a planned manoeuvre, the space probe plunged to the surface of Venus in October 1994, sending data back to Earth as it did so.

The European Space Agency's (ESA's) *Venus Express*, launched in September 2005, is currently orbiting Venus.

11

1999 MILLIONS WITNESS THE LAST TOTAL SOLAR ECLIPSE OF THE CENTURY.

A solar eclipse occurs when the moon is between the Earth and the Sun and the Moon casts a shadow on the Earth's surface. Up to 350 million people in Europe and Asia witnessed the natural phenomenon, which began over the Atlantic. The only part of mainland Britain to witness totality, the full blacking out of the Sun by the Moon, was Cornwall in south-west England. After Britain the eclipse was seen throughout Europe and Asia. The next total eclipse over mainland Britain will be in 2090.

12

1969 POLICE USE TEAR GAS AGAINST ANGRY CROWDS IN BOGSIDE, LONDONDERRY.

The Royal Ulster Constabulary used tear gas for the first time in its history after nine hours of rioting in the mainly Catholic Bogside area of Londonderry, Northern

Ireland. The shells were fired just before midnight, sending a large crowd of youths scattering in all directions.

The trouble began during the annual Apprentice Boys march. There had been numerous outbreaks of violence between Catholics and Protestants since the start of the summer marching season. The Apprentice Boys march was allowed to go ahead despite repeated warnings of trouble. The two days of rioting that followed became known as the Battle of the Bogside. The battle ended with the direct intervention from Britain in the affairs of Northern Ireland.

Internment, a law giving the Stormont government the power to indefinitely detain suspected terrorists without trial, was introduced in August 1971 and on 24 March 1972 the Stormont government was suspended and direct rule from London was imposed over Northern Ireland.

After a long and bloody dispute, claiming hundreds of lives, and fraught political negotiations over four decades, a devolved government was finally reinstated in Northern Ireland in May 2007.

13

1961 BERLIN BECOMES A DIVIDED CITY.

Troops in East Germany sealed the border between East and West Berlin with barbed-wire fences. Within days the barbed wire was replaced with concrete blocks, and the wall became a permanent structure reaching nearly 3.6 m (11.8 ft) high and 106 km (66 miles) long. The men responsible for the building of the Berlin Wall were East German leaders Erich Honecker and Egon Krenz.

After the Second World War, Nazi Germany and its capital Berlin were divided into four zones, occupied and controlled by the Allied powers. The advent of the Cold War – the period of conflict and competition between the United States and the Soviet Union – caused the French, British and American zones to be formed into the Federal Republic of Germany (including West Berlin) in 1949. The Soviet zone then formed the German Democratic Republic (including East Berlin) the same year.

On 7 November 1989, the communist government of East Germany resigned, and two days later a jubilant crowd tore down the Berlin Wall piece by piece, 28 years after it had been erected. In 1990, East and West Germany were finally reunited. Nearly 200 people died trying to cross the Berlin Wall.

1966 The start of Mao Zedong's Cultural Revolution in China, planning to destroy the country's old customs, habits, culture and thinking.

14

1947 PAKISTAN BECAME A SOVEREIGN STATE, BRINGING AN END TO BRITISH RULE THERE.

Pakistan came into being at the time of the Partition of British India in 1947 in order to create a separate homeland for India's Muslims. From independence in 1947 until 1971, Pakistan consisted of two regions – West Pakistan, in the Indus River basin, and East Pakistan, located more than 1,600 km (1,000 miles) away in the Ganges

River delta. In response to grave internal political problems, however, an independent state of Bangladesh was proclaimed in East Pakistan in 1971.

Since 1947 the territory of Jammu and Kashmir, along the western Himalayas, has been disputed between Pakistan and India, with each holding sectors. The two countries have gone to war over the territory three times, in 1948–49, 1965 and 1971.

15

1945 THE ALLIED NATIONS CELEBRATE VJ DAY.

Towards the end of the Second World War, the Allies had delivered Japan an ultimatum to surrender on 28 July 1945. When this was ignored, the US dropped atomic bombs on Hiroshima on 6 August and Nagasaki on 9 August – the same day that Soviet forces invaded Manchuria. When Japan finally gave its unconditional surrender to the Allies on the 15 August, it ended almost six years of war. There was joy and celebration around the world and to mark the end of the Second World War, 15 August was declared Victory in Japan or VJ Day.

16

1977 ROCK AND ROLL 'KING' ELVIS PRESLEY DIES.

Elvis Presley, whose singing and performance style revolutionised popular music in the 1950s, died from a heart attack. During his lifetime Presley sold more than 300 million albums and made 33 films. He became a cultural icon around the world. Thousands of fans gathered to file past Presley's body, which lay in state at his mansion, Graceland, the day after his death.

His death has been lucrative for the 'Elvis industry'. In 2005 he came top in US magazine *Forbes*' poll of 'Richest Deceased Celebrities'.

2003 Former Ugandan dictator Idi Amin dies in exile in Saudi Arabia.

17

1987 RUDOLF HESS DIES.

Rudolf Hess was among the first to join the Nazi Party in 1920 and spent time in jail with Hitler for their involvement in an attempted coup to overthrow the Bavarian government. After they were released in 1925, Hess became Hitler's personal assistant and private secretary, transcribing and partially editing Hitler's book *Mein Kampf*.

By the time war broke out between Germany and Britain in 1939, Hess was Hitler's deputy in the Nazi Party but his role subsequently became less significant than that of the military leaders Hermann Goering and Heinrich Himmler and the minister for propaganda, Joseph Goebbels. In 1941, apparently distressed by the war, he secretly flew to Scotland to try to negotiate a peace treaty with Britain. He was arrested and subsequently convicted of war crimes at the Nuremberg Trials in 1946. He was sentenced to life imprisonment at the Spandau prison in West Berlin.

18

1964 SOUTH AFRICA IS BANNED FROM THE OLYMPIC GAMES IN TOKYO.
South Africa was banned from taking part in the Eighteenth Olympic Games in Tokyo over its refusal to condemn apartheid. The International Olympic Committee (IOC) announced the decision after South Africa failed to meet an ultimatum to comply with its demands to renounce racial discrimination in sport and opposed the ban in its own country on competition between white and black athletes. South Africa was barred from the Olympics until Barcelona in 1992, following the repeal of all apartheid laws in 1991.

South Africa's apartheid policy also led to trade sanctions and a ban on cricket and rugby tours during the 1970s and 1980s.

19

1991 SOVIET PRESIDENT MIKHAIL GORBACHEV IS OVERTHROWN BY A COUP.
Soviet President Mikhail Gorbachev was overthrown after a coup by communist hardliners. He was placed under house arrest at his holiday home in the Crimea, and the new leaders, headed by former vice-president Gennady Yanayev, declared a state of emergency. Thousands of people demonstrated against the takeover, including the president of the Russian Federation, Boris Yeltsin. Less than three days after the coup, its leaders attempted to flee the country and Gorbachev was freed and returned to power.

The coup attempt brought to the surface widespread dissatisfaction with the communist system. Gorbachev's attempts at reform had improved freedom and democracy and strengthened relations with the West, but the Soviet economy was in a desperate state. By the end of 1991 the Soviet Union had been replaced by the Commonwealth of Independent States, with Boris Yeltsin as its new leader.

89

20

1940 LEON TROTSKY IS ASSASSINATED IN MEXICO.
Leon Trotsky, one of the leaders in the Russian Revolution of 1917 and later commissar of foreign affairs and of war in the Soviet Union (1917–24), was assassinated at his home in Mexico. The assassin was a Stalinist agent, Ramon Mercader, who killed Trotsky by driving the point of an ice axe into his skull.

A brilliant thinker and charismatic leader, Trotsky constituted a considerable threat to the ambitious Soviet leader Joseph Stalin. In the 1920s Trotsky lost the struggle for power in the Soviet Union that followed Vladimir Ilyich Lenin's death. Stalin emerged as the victor, and had Trotsky removed from all positions of power and exiled. Trotsky spent the rest of his life abroad, remaining the leader of anti-Stalinist opposition in exile until his assassination.

1991 The Soviet Union is disbanded.

21

1968 COMMUNISTS END THE PRAGUE SPRING.
The Prague Spring was a period of political liberalisation in Czechoslovakia starting in January 1968, when Alexander Dubcek came to power. It lasted until 21 August when the Soviet Union and its Warsaw Pact allies invaded the country. Several members of the liberal Czechoslovak leadership who had been responsible for a programme of democratic reforms were arrested, including Dubcek. All the reforms were annulled or abandoned.

The invasion drew condemnation from around the world and many western communist parties and communist Yugoslavia and Romania refused to be linked with the USSR's actions, but the West took no action.

The communists were finally ousted on 24 November 1989 and Dubcek became chairman of the new post-communist administration in what became known as the 'Velvet Revolution'.

22

1978 KENYAN PRESIDENT JOMO KENYATTA DIES.
Jomo Kenyatta was known as the founder of Kenya, the nation he had led since its independence in 1963. A member of Kenya's largest tribe, the Kikuyu, he was one of the first and best-known African nationalist leaders.

Born Johnstone Kamau, he changed his name to Kenyatta, which was Swahili for 'light of Kenya', in the 1920s. After spending 15 years in London promoting the cause of Kenyan's independence from Britain, he returned to Kenya in 1946. In 1952 he was imprisoned by the British and spent nine years in captivity. In spite of his time in prison, Kenyatta was regarded as pro-British. Under his leadership the Kenyan economy prospered, but he did not tolerate all opposition parties.

Jomo Kenyatta is still revered in Kenya and has a public holiday in October named in his honour.

23

1939 GERMANY AND THE SOVIET UNION SIGN A NON-AGGRESSION PACT.
The Hitler-Stalin Pact of 23 August 1939 was signed only days before the start of the Second World War, and divided Eastern Europe into German- and Soviet-dominated states. By signing the agreement the Soviet leader, Joseph Stalin, had hoped to keep the Soviet Union at peace with Germany and to gain time to build up the Soviet military. The German leader, Adolf Hitler, wanted an agreement with the Soviet Union so that he could invade Poland virtually unopposed by a major world power. This he did just over one week later. The non-aggression pact became null and void when Hitler attacked the Soviet Union without warning in June 1941.

24

1954 THE PRESIDENT OF BRAZIL IS FOUND DEAD.
Brazilian President Getulio Vargas committed suicide hours after resigning his post. Dr Vargas, who shot himself through the heart, left a dramatic suicide note that was broadcast on national radio two hours after his body was discovered. In it he complained that his efforts to 'liberate' the people of Brazil had been hampered by foreign interests, which he blamed for the economic crisis gripping the nation. The president's death came at a time of serious unrest in Brazil. There was soaring inflation and wage increases were not keeping pace with prices.

President Vargas seized power in a revolution of 1930, dissolving parliament and banning all political parties and trade unions. He censored the press and suppressed all opposition. He stepped down following the Second World War, but was re-elected in 1950.

Brazil's economic history has been one of boom and bust, but economic reforms in the 1990s brought some stability to the country.

1929 Palestinian leader Yasser Arafat is born.

25

1989 *VOYAGER 2* REACHES NEPTUNE.
The unmanned *Voyager 2* spacecraft sent back the first close-up pictures of Neptune and its satellite planets, over two billion miles from Earth. Neptune's blue hue, coming from the planet's mainly methane atmosphere, was clearly visible in the images. *Voyager 2* had blasted off from Cape Canaveral, Florida in August 1977. Its twin spacecraft, *Voyager 1*, was launched the following month. Between them, *Voyager 1 and 2* explored all the giant outer planets of the solar system.

Although originally designed to last just five years, both *Voyagers* are still in communication with the Earth. They are heading towards the heliopause, the boundary between the Sun's influence and interstellar space, and the eventual goal is for them to become the first spacecraft to escape the Sun's influence.

1944 The liberation of Paris, as General Charles de Gaulle, leader of the Free French, enters the city and the German Army surrenders.

26

1994 A BRITISH MAN GETS THE FIRST BATTERY-OPERATED 'BIONIC' HEART.
The man, later named as Arthur Cornhill, was fitted with an electrical pump known as a left ventricular assist device (LVAD). The pump did most of the work of the pumping chamber of the heart, the left ventricle, rather than a total replacement human heart. During the four-hour operation, the £40,000 titanium and plastic

AUGUST

LVAD was placed in the wall of the man's abdomen and connected to his heart. The pump was powered by a battery pack worn by the patient on a belt. Cornell died from kidney failure nine months after the operation.

1985 South African runner Zola Budd breaks the 5,000 metres world record.

27

1979 LORD MOUNTBATTEN, THE QUEEN'S COUSIN, IS KILLED BY AN IRA BOMB.
Lord Louis Mountbatten was killed by a bomb blast on his boat in Ireland. One of Mountbatten's twin grandsons, Nicholas (14) and Paul Maxwell (15), a local employed as a boat boy, also died in the explosion. The Irish Republican Army (IRA) claimed responsibility for carrying out the attack, saying: 'This operation is one of the discriminate ways we can bring to the attention of the English people the continuing occupation of our country.'

Lord Mountbatten, aged 79, and his family traditionally spent their summer holiday at their castle in County Sligo, north-west Ireland. Lord Mountbatten never had a bodyguard.

1980 US president Lyndon B. Johnson is born.

28

1963 US CIVIL RIGHTS CAMPAIGNER MARTIN LUTHER KING JR SPEAKS OF HIS DREAM FOR FREEDOM.
Martin Luther King Jr spearheaded a non-violent campaign against segregation and racial discrimination in the United States. As president of the Southern Christian Leadership Conference (SCLC), he first came to prominence in 1955 when he led a 382-day boycott in an attempt to end segregation on city buses.

He spoke of his dream for freedom in an address to a 250,000-strong crowd of civil rights protesters at the Lincoln Memorial in Washington, D.C. King said:

'I have a dream that my four little children will one day live in a nation where they will not be judged by the colour of their skin but by the content of their character.'

His crusade against racial discrimination was cut dramatically short when he was assassinated on 4 April 1968 in the US city of Memphis, Tennessee, aged 39.

2004 British athlete Kelly Holmes wins the 1,500 metres gold medal in Athens.

29

2005 HURRICANE KATRINA DEVASTATES NEW ORLEANS.
The category-five storm Hurricane Katrina caused unprecedented damage in the Gulf of Mexico. New Orleans, Louisiana was worst hit, but the hurricane caused severe destruction across the entire Mississippi coast and into Alabama. Up to 80 per cent

of New Orleans was flooded after defensive barriers were breached. The storm knocked out power and submerged part of the low-lying city in up to 2 m (6.6 ft) of rising water. Pumping-out began eight days after the hurricane had struck and tens of thousands of people sought shelter in New Orleans' superdome, where water and food supplies soon ran short and sanitary facilities were inadequate. Offers of aid and assistance came from around the world, but the death toll reached 1,800, with thousands more lives and livelihoods being devastated in one of the deadliest and costliest natural disasters to hit the United States.

30

1982 PLO LEADER YASSER ARAFAT IS FORCED TO LEAVE LEBANON.
The leader of the Palestine Liberation Organisation (PLO), Yasser Arafat left following the Israeli invasion of Lebanon some three months before. Israeli forces entered Lebanon after an assassination attempt on their ambassador by Palestinian dissidents. Arafat's departure was widely regarded as a heavy defeat for the Palestinians. The PLO established new headquarters in Tunis. On 16 September, Israeli-backed Christian militias entered two Palestinian refugee camps in Beirut and massacred many hundreds of Palestinians. This was in retaliation for the assassination of president-elect Bashir Gemayel four days earlier.

Years of violence followed before agreements on partial autonomy were signed between the PLO and Israel in 1993 and 1995. The Palestinian National Authority took control of the newly autonomous areas of Gaza and Jericho, with Arafat as its elected president from 1996.

Yasser Arafat died in November 2004. Following elections, Mahmoud Abbas became Palestinian president in January 2005 and called for a ceasefire between Israel and Palestinian militants.

93

31

1997 PRINCESS DIANA DIES IN A CAR CRASH IN PARIS, FRANCE.
Princess Diana, the former wife of Prince Charles and mother of Prince William and Prince Harry, died after a car crash in Paris. The accident happened after the princess left the Ritz Hotel in the French capital with her companion, Dodi Al Fayed. Al Fayed and the vehicle's driver were also killed, and only the princess's bodyguard survived. The car was being pursued at high speed by photographers on motorbikes at the time of the accident.

Diana was a revered style icon around the world. She was involved in many charities, including controversial ones such as leprosy and AIDS, where her warm, hands-on approach was credited with breaking down prejudices. There was an unprecedented national outpouring of grief at the death of the 'People's Princess'.

An initial inquest into the princess's death was opened in the UK in 2004 but was adjourned and recommenced in September 2007.

September

1

1939 GERMAN FORCES INVADE POLAND.

German forces invaded Poland and bombed Polish cities, including the capital Warsaw, in an attack that came without any warning or declaration of war. Britain and France issued separate ultimatums on 3 September 1939, demanding the withdrawal of German troops. German leader Adolf Hitler ignored the ultimatums.

During the mid-1930s, Hitler had followed a policy of mass rearmament. By late 1938, the Nazi dictator was proclaiming Germany's right to annex the Sudetenland, a Czechoslovakian territory with a significant German population. In an act of appeasement, British prime minister Neville Chamberlain signed the Munich Agreement, giving control of the Sudetenland to Germany. When the rest of Czechoslovakia was invaded in March 1939, Chamberlain warned that further attempts by Germany to expand would meet with resistance and the attack on Poland finally induced Britain and France to declare war on Germany.

2

1945 JAPAN SIGNS AN UNCONDITIONAL SURRENDER, ENDING THE SECOND WORLD WAR.

Japan's signing of an act of unconditional surrender, finally brought to an end six years of world war. Japanese envoys boarded the American battleship *Missouri* in Tokyo Bay to sign the surrender document and a convoy of 42 US ships entered Tokyo Bay and landed 13,000 American troops. Under the terms of the ceasefire, Japan agreed to end all hostilities, release all prisoners of war, and comply with the Potsdam declaration. It also agreed to acknowledge the authority of the US supreme commander, although Emperor Hirohito was allowed to remain as a symbolic head of state. Japan did not regain its independence until 1952.

Japan entered the war by attacking American naval ships at Pearl Harbor in December 1941. It had finally conceded defeat following nuclear bomb attacks on Hiroshima and Nagasaki and the Soviet declaration of war and occupation of Manchuria at the beginning of August.

3

1939 BRITAIN AND FRANCE DECLARE WAR ON GERMANY, FOLLOWING THE INVASION OF POLAND.

A few hours after the declaration of war, the British liner *Athenia* was torpedoed and sunk by a German U-boat ('Unterseeboot', or submarine). This event marked the beginning of the Battle of the Atlantic, a desperate struggle by the British to maintain what was known as the Atlantic lifeline – the shipping lanes – to North America. German submarines were a serious and ever-present threat to the British war effort. Winston Churchill once wrote that, '... *the only thing that ever really frightened me during the war was the U-boat peril'*.

If Germany had succeeded in preventing merchant ships from carrying food, raw materials, troops and their equipment from North America to Britain, the outcome of the Second World War could have been very different. Britain might have been starved into submission, and her armies would not have been equipped with American-built tanks and vehicles. Also, if the Allies had been prevented from moving ships about the North Atlantic, they would not have would have been able to send British and American troops ashore in the Mediterranean or in the D-Day landings.

1929 The Dow Jones Industrial Average peaks, followed by the Wall Street Crash.

4

1985 FIRST PICTURES OF THE *TITANIC* WRECK ARE RELEASED.

The *Titanic* wreck had been discovered three days before by a joint American-French expedition lead by the explorer Dr Robert Ballard. It had taken two ships, the assistance of the US Navy and eight weeks of searching to make the historic discovery. The ship was lying at a depth of 4 km (2.5 miles) and was filmed by an unmanned submarine called *Argo*. Dr Ballard returned the following year on a US Navy vessel and made 11 dives to the wreck. Many more expeditions have visited the *Titanic* since, despite objections from some survivors and their relatives, who believe the site should be left untouched.

The RMS *Titanic* was the largest ocean passenger liner built at the time. On her maiden voyage she tragically collided with an iceberg and sank on 15 April 1912. Over 2,200 passengers were aboard the *Titanic*, but only 712 survived. In 1997 James Cameron's hugely successful film *Titanic* was released, starring Kate Winslet and Leonardo DiCaprio.

5

1959 THE UK'S FIRST DIRECT CALL IS MADE FROM A PAY PHONE.

The UK's direct-dialling or trunk-dialling system for public phone boxes replaced the operator system payphones that had been introduced in 1925. The first direct call was made by the deputy lord mayor from a phone box in Bristol; he phoned the lord mayor of London. The new streamlined coin phone boxes were part of the Post Office's £35 million scheme to modernise the phone system and popularise use of the telephone. In 1976 the last manual exchange on the Isle of Skye closed, making the British telephone system fully automatic.

British Telecom took over the running of the phone system from the Post Office in 1981. In 1985 BT began a £160 million programme to replace the UK's famous red phone boxes with blue payphones in aluminium and stainless-steel booths.

1997 Mother Teresa, who devoted her life to helping the sick and the poor, dies at the age of 87.

6

1997 PRINCESS DIANA'S FUNERAL TAKES PLACE IN LONDON.
Following an unprecedented week of mourning, Princess Diana's took place at Westminster Abbey, London. Politicians and celebrities joined the royal family at the abbey and over one million people lined the route of the funeral cortege. Diana's sons, Princes William and Harry, joined their father Prince Charles, grandfather Prince Philip and the princess's brother Earl Spencer walking behind the coffin.

The emotional ceremony was watched by an estimated 2.5 billion people worldwide. Earl Spencer made a funeral address in which he described his sister as the *'very essence of compassion, of duty, of style, of beauty'*.

Singer Elton John played a re-worked version of his hit song 'Candle in the Wind', called 'Goodbye England's Rose'. The song, released as a tribute to Diana, went on to become the best-selling single in history. The public day of mourning ended with a private ceremony when the princess was buried on an island in the Spencer's family estate at Althorp, Northamptonshire.

7

1940 LONDON BLITZED BY GERMAN BOMBER PLANES.
The German air force's first heavy bombing raids on London killed hundreds of civilians. The first raids were concentrated on the densely populated East End, along the river by London's docks. About 300 bombers attacked the city for over an hour and a half. Once darkness fell, it is believed the light from the burning buildings guided a second wave of German bombers, for an attack lasting over eight hours.

The attacks were the first time Britain had experienced strategic bombing, when air forces aimed at civilian morale and industrial production rather than military targets. They marked the start of what came to be called the London Blitz – Adolf Hitler's attempt to crush the spirit of the British people. But the Blitz raids proved to be disastrous for the German Luftwaffe, which lost almost all its experienced aircrew and hundreds of aircraft.

About 43,000 civilians died during the Blitz. Almost 140,000 more were injured, and more than a million homes damaged or destroyed.

8

1943 ANNOUNCEMENT IS MADE THAT ITALY HAS SIGNED AN UNCONDITIONAL SURRENDER.
The surrender was signed in secret on 3 September by a representative of Marshal Pietro Badoglio, Italy's prime minister since the downfall of Benito Mussolini in July. General Eisenhower, the commander-in-chief of Allied forces in the Mediterranean, said the Italian government had agreed to end all hostilities with the United Nations.

It was agreed to keep the surrender secret until the Allied invasion of Italy was well under way.

Italy, under fascist dictator Benito Mussolini, had allied itself with Nazi Germany from 1936 and joined the Second World War in June 1940. But military defeats in the Balkans and North Africa reduced confidence in Mussolini as a leader and he was ousted in July 1943 with the king's approval. His successor, Marshal Badoglio, had resigned as chief of the supreme general staff after opposing the invasion of Greece in October 1940.

In retaliation for the Italian armistice, the Germans launched Operation Axis, which included the ruthless disarming of the Italian Army.

9

1976 CHINESE CHAIRMAN MAO ZEDONG DIES.

Chairman Mao Zedong, the chief architect of the Chinese revolution died at the age of 82. He had co-founded the Chinese Communist Party in 1921 and led the communist forces on the epic 'long march' to Shenis in northern China to flee attacks from the nationalist Kuomintang party in the mid-1930s.

In 1949 he became chairman of the newly established People's Republic of China, becoming the leader of China's 800 million citizens. During the 1950s, he launched the Great Leap Forward, a campaign to increase industrial production by mobilising China's enormous manpower into rural peoples' communes. The Cultural Revolution was launched in 1966, with schools and colleges being closed and many officials losing their jobs, being tortured and killed.

Chairman Mao's death left a power vacuum in China, with Deng Xiaoping eventually emerging as China's new leader in 1978.

10

1922 TURKISH TROOPS CAPTURE SMYRNA, MASSACRING THE GREEK POPULATION AND ENDING THE GREEK-TURKISH WAR.

After the First World War, Greece had attempted to extend its territory beyond eastern Thrace (in Europe) and the area around Smyrna (now Izmir, in western Turkey). In January 1921 the Greek Army, despite its lack of equipment and its unprotected supply lines, launched an offensive against the nationalist Turks. The Turks, commanded by the nationalist leader Mustafa Kemal, defeated the Greeks at the Sakarya River in 1921. A year later the Turks seized control of Smyrna, setting fire to the Greek, Armenian and European quarters of the city, while ensuring that no damage was done to Turkish neighbourhoods. The fires raged for two days and, amid terrible brutality and slaughter, the death toll was estimated to reach 100,000.

The Greek military collapse was total. Although he did not witness it at first hand, the writer Ernest Hemingway used the Smyrna catastrophe 14 years later in one of his short stories, 'The Snows of Kilimanjaro' (1936):

'The Turks had come steadily and lumpily and he had seen the skirted men running and the officers shooting into them and running then themselves ... Later he had seen the things that he could never think of and later still he had seen much worse.'

1943 The Italian fleet surrenders at Valetta, Malta, giving the British Royal Navy control of the Mediterranean.

11

2001 TERRORIST ATTACKS DESTROY THE WORLD TRADE CENTER IN NEW YORK CITY, USA.

A civilian airliner was hijacked by terrorists and crashed into the north tower of the World Trade Center and, minutes later, a second plane was flown into the south tower, causing another devastating explosion. The second crash was captured live on news cameras filming the burning north tower. An hour after the attack, the 110-storey south tower collapsed, with the north tower following shortly after. It took almost nine months to clear the millions of tonnes of rubble at 'Ground Zero', where the twin towers had stood.

The Pentagon was also severely damaged by a third hijacking and a fourth plane crashed in a field near Pittsburgh. An unprecedented state of emergency was declared in Washington, D.C. and the United States closed its airspace and its borders with Mexico and Canada.

The hijackers were soon linked to al-Qaeda, the Islamic militant group set up by Osama bin Laden. US president George Bush declared a worldwide 'war on terror', and on 8 October the United States and Britain hit targets in Afghanistan, where bin Laden was believed to be hiding.

Bush extended his campaign against terror in March 2003, when a coalition dominated by US and UK forces invaded Iraq.

12

1977 STEVE BIKO, LEADER OF THE BLACK CONSCIOUSNESS MOVEMENT IN SOUTH AFRICA, DIES.

Steve Biko died in police custody after being detained under the Terrorism Act on 18 August. Biko was born in the Eastern Cape of South Africa in 1946. He became active in the anti-apartheid movement in 1960s and set up the South African Students' Organisation (SASO) in 1968. He was elected its first president the following year. In 1972 he began working for the Black Community Programmes (BCP), and in 1977 he was made its honorary president.

Biko's death caused outrage in South Africa. Biko's close friend and newspaper editor Donald Woods accused the minister of justice and police, James Kruger, of being directly responsible for the death. The inquest in November 1977 cleared the police of any wrongdoing, but after the election of the ANC government in 1994, the Truth and Reconciliation Commission found that Biko's death had been a direct result of injuries he sustained in custody. Biko's contribution to the black fight for freedom from apartheid was dramatised in the film *Cry Freedom*.

2005 England's cricketers beat Australia to win the Ashes series for the first time since 1987.

13

1993 HISTORIC HANDSHAKE BETWEEN ISRAELI PRIME MINISTER YITZHAK RABIN AND PLO LEADER YASSER ARAFAT.
The prime minister of Israel, Yitzhak Rabin, and the leader of the Palestinian Liberation Organisation (PLO), Yasser Arafat, shook hands in front of the White House in Washington, D.C. This marked the signing of a Declaration of Principles for peace between the Arabs and Israelis. Israel agreed to withdraw its troops from the Gaza Strip and West Bank by April 1994. Elections would then be held in the territories to allow the Palestinians a form of self-government.

Following the Declaration came Israel's first withdrawals from occupied territory and Arafat's return from exile to Palestinian territory in July 1994. He was elected president of the Palestinian National Authority in 1996. Rabin was assassinated on 4 November 1995 by a Jewish extremist wanting to prevent further Israeli withdrawals.

14

1960 THE ORGANISATION OF THE PETROLEUM EXPORTING COUNTRIES – OPEC – IS FOUNDED IN BAGHDAD.
OPEC is a multinational organisation that was established to coordinate the petroleum policies of its members and to provide member states with technical and economic aid. It was founded on 14 September 1960 and formally constituted in January 1961 by five countries: Saudi Arabia, Iran, Iraq, Kuwait and Venezuela. It later included among its members Qatar, Indonesia, Libya, Algeria, the United Arab Emirates, Nigeria and Angola. OPEC members collectively own about two-thirds of the world's proven petroleum reserves and account for two-fifths of world oil production.

1917 Russia is declared a republic.

15

1940 VICTORY FOR THE RAF IN THE BATTLE OF BRITAIN.
Britain's Royal Air Force (RAF) claimed victory over the German Luftwaffe after a day of heavy bombing raids ended in big losses on the side of the enemy. The first big German attack came in the morning when about 100 German aircraft headed over the Kent coast towards London. RAF Spitfire and Hurricane squadrons were sent to meet them and many German planes reportedly turned away without dropping any bombs. The attacks continued throughout the day and night, with a series of smaller raids inflicting damage on major targets across the south of England.

Air raids continued over London and the south-east of England into October, but the Germans were losing planes faster than they could replace them and consequently switched to less successful night-time raids. In 1940, Hitler indefinitely postponed

Operation Sealion, his plan to invade Britain. In total the RAF claimed to have shot down 2,698 German planes during the Battle of Britain, but the actual figure was closer to 1,300. The RAF lost 788 planes, which was far fewer than the 3,058 the Luftwaffe claimed.

1964 The *Sun*, a British tabloid newspaper, is published for the first time.

16

1992 BRITAIN DROPS OUT OF THE EUROPEAN EXCHANGE RATE MECHANISM (ERM).
On a day that was to become known as 'Black Wednesday', the British government suspended its membership of the European Exchange Rate Mechanism. All that day the UK's prime minister and chancellor had tried to prop up a failing pound; ultimately their only way forward was to withdraw from the monetary system the country had joined two years earlier.

Membership of the ERM meant that a country had to agree to keep its currency value within set limits which were linked to the German mark. As a consequence, member countries were forced to adopt the anti-inflation policies of the German Bundesbank. Membership of the ERM was a condition of joining the Euro – Europe's single currency.

1963 The Federation of Malaysia is formed.

17

1978 THE CAMP DAVID ACCORDS ARE CONCLUDED.
The Camp David Accords, negotiated by US president Jimmy Carter, were completed leading to a peace treaty between Egypt and Israel and a broader framework for pursuing peace in the Middle East. The agreements were signed by Israeli prime minister Menachem Begin and Egyptian President Anwar el-Sadat at the US presidential retreat at Camp David in rural Maryland in the USA.

1939 The Soviet Union invades Poland, having made a secret agreement with Nazi Germany.

18

1931 THE JAPANESE BEGIN THEIR INVASION OF MANCHURIA, CHINA.
On the night of 18 September, the Japanese Army used the pretext of an explosion along the Japanese-controlled South Manchurian Railway to occupy Mukden, a city in Manchuria. Throughout the early twentieth century the Japanese had maintained special rights in Manchuria; they had felt that the neutrality of the area was necessary for the defence of their colony in Korea. The unification of China in the late 1920s alarmed the Japanese, as did the increasing pressure from the Soviet Union to the

north. Responding to this pressure, Japanese army officers initiated the incident in Mukden without the approval of the civil government of Japan.

The Mukden incident led to the expansion of the Japanese Army throughout Manchuria, an occupation that continued until Japan's defeat by the Allies in 1945, at the end of the Second World War.

1997 Voters in Wales narrowly approve the creation of a Welsh assembly in a national referendum.

19

1985 MEXICO IS HIT BY A DEVASTATING EARTHQUAKE.
The massive earthquake hit Mexico not far from its capital, Mexico City. It was measured by the US Geological Survey at a magnitude of 7.8 and lasted for 50 seconds. A massive aftershock hit the city just one day later, increasing the terrible damage caused by the first tremor. Mexico City, which has a population of around 18 million was declared a disaster zone. More than 10,000 people were killed in the quake, 30,000 were injured, and large parts of the city were destroyed. About 6,000 buildings were flattened and quarter of a million people lost their homes.

Mexico City remains at risk from earthquakes, as it sits on an old lake-bed, which amplifies seismic waves. During the massive reconstruction of the city, buildings were strengthened to help them withstand tremors.

101

20

1970 A SOVIET SPACE PROBE LANDS ON THE MOON.
The Russian space probe *Luna 16* landed on the Moon to collect samples from its surface. It was the first time an unmanned probe had been used to bring objects back to Earth from space. It collected samples of rock and dust using an electric drill at the end of a mechanical extendable arm to cut small cores from just under the topsoil. The probe was also equipped with a television camera. *Luna 16* successfully returned to Earth on 24 September. It carried about 100 g (3.5 oz) of lunar soil and rock. The probe left an experimental station on the surface of the Moon, which continued to send back data to Earth.

The previous year, NASA's successful *Apollo 11* mission had made history when Neil Armstrong became the first man to land safely on the Moon.

21

1931 THE BANK OF ENGLAND DROPS THE GOLD STANDARD.
As a result of the Bank of England's decision to drop the gold standard, the pound sterling lost 28 per cent of its value, which undermined the economies of countries in Eastern Europe and South America.

The gold standard linked nearly all the countries of the world in a network of fixed currency exchange rates. Under it, each country set the value of its currency in terms of gold and took monetary actions to defend the fixed price. It played an important part in transmitting the American economic downturn of the 1930s, known as the Great Depression, to other countries. The economic impact of the Great Depression was enormous, causing drastic declines in output, severe unemployment, and acute deflation in almost every country of the world.

1937 J. R. R. Tolkien's fantasy tale *The Hobbit* is published.

22

1980 WAR BREAKS OUT BETWEEN IRAN AND IRAQ.

After three weeks of border clashes between Iran and Iraq, all-out war erupted on 22 September 1980. Iraq bombed several Iranian air and military supply bases, including Tehran's international airport, and her armed forces invaded western Iran along the countries' joint border.

The roots of the war lay in a number of territorial and political disputes between Iraq and Iran. Iraq's superior military equipment initially gave it the upper hand in the fighting, but Iran fought back and, by December 1980, the Iraqi offensive had stalled. The Iran-Iraq war rumbled on for eight years, but in August 1988 Iran's deteriorating economy and recent Iraqi gains on the battlefield compelled it to accept a United Nations-mediated ceasefire that it had previously resisted. Official reports say more than 400,000 had been killed and 750,000 wounded in the fighting.

Iraq's international reputation was damaged during the war by reports that it had used lethal chemical weapons against Iranian troops and, in Iraq itself, against Kurdish civilians whom the Iraqi government thought to be sympathetic to Iran.

1980 The Polish trade union and political party Solidarity is formed.

23

1942 BRIGADIER GENERAL LESLIE GROVES TAKES OVER THE 'MANHATTAN PROJECT' TO CREATE AN ATOMIC BOMB.

On 23 September 1942, Brigadier General Leslie R. Groves was put in charge of the US government's 'Manhattan Project' to develop an atomic bomb. The project was developed because reports coming through from Germany suggested that Nazi scientists were pushing ahead with an atom-bomb project, and the United States therefore decided to push ahead strongly with its own programme.

In June 1942, the US atomic bomb project was moved to the War Department's Army Corps of Engineers. A Manhattan Engineer District was created by the Corps to disguise the project, with its headquarters based, initially, in New York City. The 'Manhattan Project' employed nearly 129,000 people. All these workers were required to build, run and maintain the huge industrial facilities that were needed to create an atomic bomb.

Ultimately the 'Manhattan Project' was a success. Two bombs were built: the 'Little Boy' and the 'Fat Man'. In 1945, 'Little Boy' was dropped on the Japanese city of Hiroshima and 'Fat Man' was dropped on Nagasaki – both of them to devastating and terrible effect.

2000 British rower Steve Redgrave makes Olympic history at the Sydney Games by winning his fifth consecutive gold medal.

1939 Sigmund Freud, the founder of modern psychoanalysis, dies in London.

24

1957 FEDERAL TROOPS ARE SENT IN TO LITTLE ROCK, ARKANSAS, USA.
On the orders of President Dwight D. Eisenhower, US federal troops arrived in Little Rock on the evening of 24 September. In full battle dress, and with fixed bayonets and rifles, they took over from local police following three weeks of disturbances. Under this armed escort, the following morning nine black students were finally able to attend the all-white Central High School. But they needed the US paratroopers to protect them from a crowd of around 1,500 segregationist whites who were demonstrating outside the building.

25

1970 HOSTILITIES COME TO AN END DURING BLACK SEPTEMBER.
In September 1970 in Jordan, tensions between the army loyal to King Hussein and Palestinian guerrillas erupted in a brief but bloody civil war that became known as 'Black September'.
The crisis began when Palestinian guerrillas hijacked four aircraft and took three of them to a remote desert airstrip, Dawson's Field in Jordan. One of their commanders, Leila Khaled, was being held in London. Demanding her release, the hijackers blew up the three airliners, having released almost all the hostages amid behind-the-scenes negotiations with the UK and other governments. When the Jordanian army moved against the guerrillas, however, war broke out. Hostilities formally ended on 25 September. Total casualties were variously estimated at 1,000 to 5,000 people killed and up to 10,000 injured.

26

1960 KENNEDY AND NIXON CLASH IN THE FIRST TELEVISED US PRESIDENTIAL DEBATE.
More than 60 million Americans tuned in to watch the first-ever televised debate between the two candidates running for the White House – Democrat John F. Kennedy and Republican vice-president Richard Nixon. The two men appeared in a studio in Chicago, Illinois, for the first of a series of four debates.

The first debate focused on domestic issues. Each candidate was given eight minutes to make an opening speech. There followed a question-and-answer session, and then each man was allowed three minutes and 20 seconds for a final statement. When canvassed, TV viewers overwhelmingly thought the tanned and youthful Kennedy gave a better performance than the pale and stressed Nixon.

27

1918 BRITISH FORCES ATTACK THE HINDENBURG LINE.
In the final offensive on the Western Front during the First World War, the British attacked the Hindenburg Line, a defensive barrier set up by the German Army. The Line was punctuated by concrete pillboxes manned by soldiers armed with machine guns; it had resisted all Allied attacks in 1917. The British offensive, which took place between Cambrai and Saint-Quentin on 27 September, threatened the Germans' line of retreat and unnerved the German supreme command.

1960 British suffragette Sylvia Pankhurst dies.

1996 Taliban leaders seize the capital city of Kabul, declaring the whole of Afghanistan an Islamic state.

28

1989 PHILIPPINES DICTATOR FERDINAND MARCOS DIES IN EXILE.
The death of Ferdinand Marcos in Honolulu, Hawaii, marked the end of an era in Philippines politics characterised by corruption, injustice, repression, political murders and a huge rich-poor divide. As president of the Phillippines, Marcos's regime spanned 20 years, from 1966 to 1986, and earned him the reputation of a ruthless dictator at home and abroad. Although his fierce opposition to Communism won him enthusiastic support from the US government of the time, he encountered ongoing violent leftist opposition to his rule in his own country. In 1986, he was finally hounded from office by the supporters of Corazon Aquino, the wife of rival allegedly assassinated on Marcos's instructions. Marcos and his wife, Imelda, a former beauty queen, fled to Hawaii in exile.

1964 The US government-commissioned Warren Report finds that the murder of John F. Kennedy was 'no conspiracy'.

29

1913 GIFTED INVENTOR THROWS HIMSELF OFF CROSS-CHANNEL CRUISE BOAT.
Rudolf Diesel, the man best known for inventing the internal-combustion engine that bears his name, jumped to his death from the deck of a cruiser in the English

Channel. The high efficiency of Diesel's engine, together with its comparative simplicity of design, made it an immediate commercial success. The diesel engine changed the world; it was more efficient than steam, and was used on everything from trains to boats, eventually revolutionising the car later in the twentieth century. A hugely talented man, Diesel was not only an engineer – he was also a linguist, a social theorist and a connoisseur of the arts.

30

1938 THE MUNICH AGREEMENT IS SIGNED.
In a last-minute attempt to avoid war, Britain and France agreed to sign an agreement in Munich, Germany. The settlement, reached by Germany, Britain, France and Italy, gave Germany permission to annex the Sudetenland, an area of western Czechoslovakia. None of the signatories had asked the Czechs or their government for their views on this move. Britain and France subsequently told Czechoslovakia that it could either resist Germany alone or submit to the annexation. Not surprisingly the Czech government chose to submit.

Before leaving Munich, Chamberlain and Hitler signed a further paper, which agreed that they would resolve their differences through consultation to assure peace. In Britain, Chamberlain was welcomed home by jubilant crowds relieved that the threat of war had passed. Chamberlain told the British public that he had achieved *'peace with honour. I believe it is peace in our time.'* The Second World War broke out in September of the following year.

1955 American motion picture actor James Dean dies in car crash in Paso Robles, California.

105

October

1

1908 THE FIRST MODEL T FORD AUTOMOBILE IS BUILT.
At the start of the twentieth century, US industrialist Henry Ford dreamed of building a car for use by the masses. The vehicle he had in mind, the Model T Ford, was first assembled at the Piquette Avenue Plant in Detroit on 1 October 1908. Over the next 19 years Ford would build 15,000,000 automobiles with the Model T engine – the longest run of any single model apart from the Volkswagen Beetle. From 1908 to 1927 the sturdy, low-priced Model T continued to be produced with little change in its design, and Henry Ford's company became the biggest in the industry.

By 1914, the moving assembly line enabled Ford to produce far more cars than any other company. The Model T and mass production made Ford an international celebrity. It is not altogether certain that Ford uttered the famous words: '*You can have it in any colour ... so long as it's black*', but the phrase has entered the common language as a tribute to the unfussy and reliably unalterable character of the Model T Ford.

1949 Communist leader Mao Zedong proclaims the establishment of the People's Republic of China.

2

1935 FASCIST DICTATOR MUSSOLINI INVADES ABYSSINIA.
By 1935, Benito Mussolini had ruled Italy for 13 years but had made little progress toward the 'new Roman Empire' he believed would free Italy from the 'prison of the Mediterranean'. His conviction was that only full-scale war could fully undermine the monarchy and the church in Italy and bring about the fascist revolution at home. The ambitious Mussolini lighted on North Africa, and Abyssinia (Ethiopia) in particular, as a good place to start expanding his horizons.

On 2 October 1935, Italian forces led by fascist loyalist Emilio De Bono invaded the independent African country of Abyssinia. In 1896 Italy had failed to conquer Abyssinia, so Mussolini thought he could now erase the memory of a national humiliation. Abyssinia also boasted fertile uplands and abundant raw materials suitable for Italy's excess rural population, and it would open the path for conquering further lands in the Sudan and beyond.

1911 Francisco Madero is elected president of Mexico.

3

1990 GERMANY IS REUNIFIED.

When communist regimes in the Soviet-bloc countries of Eastern Europe collapsed in 1989–90, four decades of Cold War division and hostility came to an end. The fall of the communist regimes prompted the rise to power of democratic governments in East Germany, Poland, Hungary and Czechoslovakia. In July 1990, the German chancellor Helmut Kohl persuaded the Soviet leader Mikhail Gorbachev to agree to the unification of East and West Germany in exchange for German financial aid to the Soviet Union. The unification treaty came into effect on 3 October 1990.

1995 American football player O. J. Simpson is found not guilty of the murders of his ex-wife Nicole and her friend Ronald Goldman.

4

1957 *SPUTNIK 1* SATELLITE BLASTS INTO SPACE.

The Soviet Union launched *Sputnik 1*, the first man-made object ever to leave the Earth's atmosphere. *Sputnik 1* was an 83.6-kg (184-lb) capsule. It achieved an Earth orbit with an apogee (furthest point from Earth) of 940 km (584 miles) and a perigee (nearest point) of 230 km (143 miles). It circled the Earth every 96 minutes and remained in orbit until early 1958, when it fell back and burned in the Earth's atmosphere. The launch of *Sputnik 1* heralded the space age and heightened Cold War competition between the Soviet Union and the United States.

107

5

1947 THE FIRST PRESIDENTIAL SPEECH ON TELEVISION.

President Harry S. Truman made the first televised presidential address from the White House in Washington, D.C. At the time of Truman's speech, Europe was still recovering from the Second World War and suffering hardship and famine. The president asked the American people to buy only what they needed and to cut back on their food consumption so that extra food could be sent to their European allies. But unfortunately the majority of US citizens missed seeing Truman's speech as television was still in its infancy and very few people owned a set!

1936 Václav Havel, writer, poet and president of Czechoslovakia (1989-92) and the Czech Republic (1993-2003) is born in Prague.

6

1973 THE YOM KIPPUR WAR BEGINS.

On the Jewish holy day of Yom Kippur, heavy fighting began between Arab and Israeli forces and Israel suffered heavy casualties. To the south, Egyptian armoured forces broke the Israeli line on the eastern bank of the Suez Canal. In the north, Syrian troops and tanks battled with Israeli defences along the Golan Heights, an area seized by Israel from Syria in 1967. Both sides accused each other of firing the first shots, but UN observers reported seeing Egyptian and Syrian troops crossing into Israeli-held territory. Eventually the Israeli army reversed its early losses, pushed into Syrian territory and encircled the Egyptian 3rd Army by crossing the Suez Canal and establishing forces on its west bank. Israel and Egypt signed a ceasefire agreement in November 1973 and peace agreements on 18 January 1974.

1927 The first 'talking picture', *The Jazz Singer*, starring Al Jolson, premieres in New York City, introducing the sound era of motion pictures.

7

2001 THE USA LAUNCHES AIR STRIKES AGAINST THE TALIBAN.
The United States began a military campaign, Operation Enduring Freedom, against Islamic militant group al-Qaeda and the Taliban in Afghanistan. Cruise missiles and bombers targeted the airports of Kandahar and Kabul, and terrorist training camps near Jalalabad. The attacks were the first retaliatory response to the 11 September 2001 terror attacks in the United States, in which nearly 3,000 people died. US President George W. Bush promised a 'sustained and relentless' campaign, with the objectives of stopping Afghanistan from remaining a terrorist haven and finding al-Qaeda leader Osama bin Laden.

Within three months, the Taliban had been ousted from government in Afghanistan, but bin Laden remained at large. Estimates of civilian deaths in Afghanistan varied between several hundred and several thousand.

8

1967 SOUTH AMERICAN REBEL LEADER CHE GUEVARA IS CAPTURED.
A prominent communist figure and guerrilla leader, Che Guevara was captured in Bolivia and subsequently shot to death by members of the Bolivian Army. In his early life, Guevara's observations of the great poverty of many Latin-American people had convinced him that the only solution to their problems lay in violent revolution. He became an expert in guerrilla warfare, and fought alongside Fidel Castro in his rise to power in the Cuban Revolution of the late 1950s. In the autumn of 1966, Guevara went to Bolivia to create and lead a guerrilla group in the region of Santa Cruz. On 8 October 1967, the group was almost wiped out by a special detachment of the Bolivian Army. Guevara, who was wounded in the attack, was captured and shot.

After his execution, he came to be regarded as a martyred hero by generations of students and leftists worldwide. His image – on posters, leaflets and T-shirts – has become one of the most familiar icons of the late twentieth century.

1957 An accident at the Windscale nuclear facility in north-western England causes a fire that burns for 16 hours and leaves 10 tonnes of radioactive fuel melted in the reactor core.

9

1936 THE HOOVER DAM BEGINS TO POWER LOS ANGELES, USA.
By harnessing the power of the mighty Colorado River, the Hoover Dam began sending electricity over transmission lines spanning 428 km (266 miles) of mountains and deserts to run the lights, radios and stoves of Los Angeles.

Initially named the Boulder Dam, work on the dam was begun under President Herbert Hoover's administration but completed during the Roosevelt administration (which renamed it for Hoover). When it was finished in 1935, the towering concrete and steel structure was the tallest dam in the world. In fact, the electricity generated deep in the base of the Hoover Dam was only a secondary benefit. The main reason for the dam was the collection, preservation and distribution of water.

1988 Thousands of people in the country of Latvia begin a mass movement to press Moscow for greater independence from the Soviet Union.

10

1980 EARTHQUAKES STRIKE ALGERIA.
Two big earthquakes hit the northern Algerian town of El Asnam. An official report said that up to 20,000 people had died and many tens of thousands were injured or missing. The main hospital, a big department store, the central mosque, a girls' school and two housing complexes were destroyed. There were a number of aftershocks after the first two quakes, which sent more refugees fleeing to the relative safety of the countryside. Mountain sniffer dogs from the French and Swiss Alps were brought in to help look for survivors beneath the rubble – a number of whom were found. The final death toll was around 3,500 – much lower than the original prediction. El Asnam was subsequently rebuilt and renamed Chlef.

1917 One of the first creators of modern jazz, American pianist and composer Thelonious Monk, is born.

11

1987 THE SEARCH FOR THE LOCH NESS MONSTER IS CALLED OFF.
Loch Ness, the greatest expanse of fresh water in Europe, is world famous for sightings of 'Nessie', the Loch Ness Monster. Most witnesses have described the creature as having a long neck, which has given rise to the theory that there might be a prehistoric reptile – a plesiosaur – living in the lake. However, a major sonar exploration of Loch Ness in Scotland was abandoned as scientists failed to find any trace of the monster.

2000 The title Greatest Woman Achiever of the Century is awarded to Russian cosmonaut Valentina Tereshkova – the first woman in space.

109

12

2002 HUNDREDS ARE KILLED IN A NIGHTCLUB EXPLOSION ON BALI.
More than 200 people were killed in two explosions on the Indonesian holiday island of Bali. The attack killed 164 foreign nationals and 38 Indonesian citizens; 209 people were injured. Three bombs were detonated in total: a backpack-mounted device carried by a suicide bomber and a large car bomb, both of which were detonated in or near popular nightclubs in Kuta; and a third, much smaller device detonated outside the United States consulate in Denpasar, causing only minor damage. Most of those killed were western holiday-makers in their twenties and thirties, including tourists from Australia, the United States, Britain and Europe. Members of the regional Islamist group Jemaah Islamiah (JI), were convicted in relation to the bombings, including three individuals who were sentenced to death.

1935 The opera singer Luciano Pavarotti is born in Modena, Italy.

13

1988 THE SHROUD OF TURIN IS RADIOCARBON DATED.
The Shroud of Turin is a linen cloth bearing the image of a man who appears to have been crucified. It is kept in the royal chapel of the Cathedral of Saint John the Baptist in Turin, Italy. The shroud is the subject of intense debate among some scientists, people of faith, historians and writers regarding where, when and how the shroud and its images were created. Some believe it is the cloth that covered Jesus of Nazareth when he was placed in his tomb, and that his image was recorded on its fibres at or near the time of his resurrection. Other people think the shroud is a medieval hoax or forgery. In 1988 scientists at three research centres carried out radiocarbon dating tests on tiny portions taken from the corner of the shroud. All three centres produced their results independently of one another. On 13 October, the archbishop of Turin announced that the radiocarbon tests indicated that the Shroud of Turin dates only to the Middle Ages (1260–1390), though its origins remain controversial.

1943 Italy declares war on Nazi Germany.

14

1912 FORMER US PRESIDENT THEODORE ROOSEVELT IS SHOT IN MILWAUKEE.
Theodore Roosevelt was shot at close range immediately before he was scheduled to make a campaign speech in Milwaukee, Wisconsin, USA. The former president was greeting the public in front of the Gilpatrick Hotel when saloonkeeper John Schrank aimed his gun at Roosevelt's heart. The bullet would almost certainly have killed its victim, but its force was slowed by a glasses case and a bundle of

manuscript in the breast pocket of Roosevelt's heavy coat – a manuscript containing Roosevelt's evening speech. Schrank was immediately arrested and reportedly offered his motive: *'Any man looking for a third term ought to be shot'.* Roosevelt survived the attack, delivered his speech, but was beaten to the presidency by Democrat Woodrow Wilson.

1944 Distinguished German field marshal Erwin Rommel, known as the 'Desert Fox', commits suicide when it is discovered that he is involved in a conspiracy to assassinate Adolf Hitler.

15

1934 CHINESE COMMUNISTS BEGIN THE LONG MARCH.
The Long March was a 10,000-km (6,000-mile) trek by Chinese communists, from south-eastern to north-western China. On 15 October 1934, on the point of being routed by nationalist forces on the Kiangsi-Fukien border, the communists fled westward. They crossed 18 mountain ranges and 24 rivers to reach the north-western province of Shensi, in a journey that took 368 days. Along they way they suffered air bombardments and ground attacks by nationalist forces, as well as disease and starvation. More than half of the marchers died before reaching their destination. The heroism of the communist troops who undertook the Long March inspired many young Chinese to join the Chinese Communist Party during the late 1930s and early 1940s.

1987 A military coup in Burkina Faso in western Africa overthrows head of state Thomas Sankara, killing him and eight others.

111

16

1987 HURRICANE WINDS BATTER SOUTHERN ENGLAND.
Southern Britain began a massive £1 billion clear-up operation following the worst night of storms in living memory. Around 15 million trees were uprooted and lost and hundreds of thousands of homes were without power for more than a day. Eighteen people died and hundreds were injured, mostly by falling trees and buildings. Rescue workers faced an unprecedented number of call-outs as winds reached speeds of 151 km/h (94 mph) in London and over 177 km/h (110 mph) in the Channel Islands.
    The worst-affected areas were along the south coast. In Kent five people died, including two seamen in Dover Harbour, and in Dorset two firemen were killed while out on an emergency call. Weather forecasters were accused of failing to predict the severity of the weather. By the time people went to bed on 15 October, no mention of the very high winds had been made on television or radio broadcasts.

1964 China, eager to join the nuclear race, successfully detonates its first atomic bomb.

17

1968 OLYMPIC ATHLETES MAKE SILENT PROTEST.

Two black US athletes made history at the Mexico Olympics by staging a silent protest against racial discrimination. Tommie Smith and John Carlos, gold and bronze medallists in the 200 metres, stood with their heads bowed, each with a black-gloved hand raised as the American national anthem played during the victory ceremony. The pair wore black socks and no shoes and Smith wore a black scarf around his neck. They said the gesture was a tribute to their African-American heritage and a protest against the living conditions of minorities in the United States. As they left the podium at the end of the ceremony they were booed by many in the crowd; both athletes were banned from the Olympic Village and sent home.

1979 Mother Teresa, founder of a Roman Catholic order of women dedicated to the poor and particularly to the destitute of India, is awarded the Nobel Prize for Peace.

18

1922 THE BBC IS BORN.

In 1922 the British Broadcasting Company Ltd was established as a private corporation, in which only British manufacturers were allowed to hold shares. In 1927 it was replaced by the British Broadcasting Corporation (BBC), a public corporation. Although it is ultimately answerable to the British parliament, the BBC has virtually complete independence in the way in which it carries out its activities.

An important figure in the early history of the BBC was John Reith (later Lord Reith), general manager from 1922 and director-general from 1927 to 1938. Under Reith, the BBC's coverage of the General Strike of 1926 gave all sides of the dispute, including that of trades union leaders. This angered the British government, as the unions were in conflict with it at the time. Reith described the BBC's purpose in three words – 'to educate, inform and entertain' – which remain part of the organisation's mission statement to this day.

1961 The movie version of the Broadway musical *West Side Story*, featuring music and lyrics by Leonard Bernstein and Stephen Sondheim, opens at New York's Rivoli Theatre.

19

1989 THE GUILDFORD FOUR ARE RELEASED AFTER 15 YEARS OF IMPRISONMENT.

In 1975, Gerry Conlon, Paul Hill, Paddy Armstrong and Carole Richardson were sentenced to life in prison. They had been found guilty of planting terrorist bombs in two pubs – one in Guildford, Surrey and another in Woolwich, London. The bombs exploded on 5 October 1974, killing seven people in total.

The Guildford Four were eventually released from prison in 1989, when an investigation concluded that the arresting Surrey police had given misleading evidence. As he emerged from the court, Conlon announced to the waiting crowds: *'I have been in prison for something I did not do. I am totally innocent.'*

The investigation into the case, considered to be the biggest miscarriage of justice in Britain, was carried out by Avon and Somerset Police.

20

1973 SYDNEY OPERA HOUSE OPENS.

In a city where there used to be a shortage of cultural venues, the monumental Opera House in Sydney, Australia was opened by Queen Elizabeth II on this day in 1973. Designed by Danish architect Jørn Utzon, whose dynamic and imaginative plan won an international competition in 1957, the Opera House rapidly became the most famous building in Australia. Built on a magnificent site on the harbour, surrounded by water on three sides, it contains a concert hall, a large theatre for opera and ballet, three smaller theatres for plays, dance, lectures, seminars and music, and a reception hall.

1968 Jacqueline Kennedy, widow of assassinated US president John F. Kennedy, marries Greek shipping magnate Aristotle Onassis.

21

1966 A COAL TIP BURIES CHILDREN IN ABERFAN, WALES.

More than 140 people, most of them children, were buried by a rain-soaked coal slag heap at the mining village of Aberfan near Merthyr Tydfil in Wales. One hundred and sixteen children died when the tip engulfed a school, some terraced cottages and a farm in just five minutes. The National Coal Board (NCB) said that abnormal rainfall had caused the coal waste to move. An inquiry later found that the NCB was wholly to blame and should pay compensation for loss and personal injuries.

The NCB and the British government treasury refused to accept full financial responsibility for the tragedy so the Aberfan Disaster Fund had to contribute £150,000 towards removing the remaining tip that overlooked the village. This amount was finally repaid in 1997 on the instigation of Ron Davies, secretary of state for Wales at the time.

22

1962 PRESIDENT KENNEDY ANNOUNCES A BLOCKADE DURING THE CUBAN MISSILE CRISIS.

The Cuban missile crisis was a major confrontation that brought the United States and the Soviet Union to the brink of nuclear war. In 1960, the Soviet Union had agreed to give military support to the communist-governed island of Cuba. In 1962, the United States learned that Soviets had begun shipping missiles to Cuba. If launched from Cuba, such missiles could hit much of the eastern United States within a few minutes.

On 22 October 1962, President John F. Kennedy alerted Americans to the Cuban missile crisis, and declared a naval blockade to prevent further missile shipments. After several extremely tense days, the Soviet Union backed down and agreed to remove the missiles. In return, the USA promised never to invade Cuba.

1934 Violent bank robber Charles ('Pretty Boy') Floyd is gunned down in a field near East Liverpool, Ohio by FBI agents.

23

1956 HUNGARIANS RISE UP AGAINST SOVIET RULE.
The Hungarian Revolution began with a massive demonstration by students in Budapest. Tens of thousands of people joined the students and took to the streets to demand an end to Soviet rule. Although the day started with a peaceful rally it ended with running battles between police and demonstrators. On 25 October, Soviet tanks opened fire on a crowd in Parliament Square at point-blank range. The people rallied and for a while it seemed as though the demonstrators and democracy would triumph, but on 4 November Soviet forces entered Budapest and began putting down the revolution.

It took many weeks for the Soviets to bring Hungary to heel, and the price in human lives was great. The Hungarians suffered about 20,000 casualties, among them some 2,500 deaths, while the Soviet losses consisted of about 1,250 wounded and more than 650 dead. Hungary remained under Soviet control until the collapse of Communism in 1989.

2002 Armed Chechen militants storm the Moscow Theatre and take 850 people hostage; around 200 die in the siege that follows.

24

1945 UNITED NATIONS IS ESTABLISHED.
The United Nations – an international organisation established to maintain world peace and friendly relations among different countries – came into being this day in 1945. Following the Second World War, 50 countries signed up to the United Nations Charter agreeing to intervene in conflicts between nations and thereby avoid war. The five permanent members of the UN Security Council, each of which has veto power on any Security Council resolution, were the main victors of the Second World War or their successor states: the People's Republic of China, France, Russia, the United Kingdom and the United States.

2003 The legendary aircraft Concorde makes its final transatlantic flight, ending 27 years of supersonic history.

25

1983 US TROOPS INVADE GRENADA.
The world was shocked when US troops invaded the tiny Caribbean island of Grenada, seized the country's two airports and took Cuban and Soviet prisoners. US president Ronald Reagan gave troops the go-ahead following a bloody coup by Cuban-trained military personnel who executed Grenada's prime minister, Maurice Bishop, and at least 13 of his associates. Reagan said the invasion was necessary to prevent the country from becoming a dangerous Soviet outpost and to protect American students at the medical school there.

The US sent in hundreds more troops over the next few days. Heavy fighting continued but as the invasion force grew to more than 7,000 the defenders either surrendered or fled into the mountains. World leaders were outraged by the actions of the United States. On 28 October the United Nations failed to get a motion passed deploring the invasion, because it was vetoed by the United States.

1917 Revolution in Russia: the Bolshevik Party, led by Vladimir Ilyich Lenin, and the workers' Soviets, overthrow the provisional government and bring about a dramatic change in the social structure of Russia that paves the way for the creation of the Soviet Union.

26

1994 ISRAEL AND JORDAN MAKE PEACE.
Israeli prime minister Yitzhak Rabin and King Hussein of Jordan formally made peace at a ceremony in the desert area of Wadi Araba on the Israeli-Jordanian border. US president Bill Clinton witnessed the signing of the treaty, which ended 46 years of war between the two countries. On 4 November 1995, Yitzhak Rabin was assassinated by a Jewish extremist and in 1999 King Hussein of Jordan died of cancer. Israeli prime minister Shimon Peres pushed on with Rabin's efforts to make peace with the Palestinians, but in 1996 he was voted out of office. Nevertheless, the peace deal struck between Israel and Jordan in 1994 continues to this day.

1958 America's first jet airliner, the Boeing 707, enters service for Pan American World Airways.

27

1945 FERDINAND PORSCHE IS ARRESTED FOR NAZI CONNECTIONS.
Following the end of the Second World War, car designer Ferdinand Porsche was arrested by US military officials for his pro-Nazi activities. In 1934, Porsche had submitted a design proposal to Adolf Hitler's government, calling for the construction of a small, simple and reliable car that the average German could afford.

The design was to become the Volkswagen ('people's car'). The first completed model was introduced in 1938, but the outbreak of the Second World War prevented mass production of the car, and the newly constructed Volkswagen factory turned to war production, constructing military vehicles such as the lethal 'Tiger' tank.

After the war, Porsche, like other German industrialists who participated in the German war effort, was investigated on war-crime charges. He was sent to France, where he was imprisoned for two years before being released. Meanwhile, the Allies approved the continuation of the original Volkswagen programme, and Volkswagen went on to become a highly successful automobile company.

1914 The author and poet Dylan Thomas is born in Swansea, South Wales.

28

1914 JONAS EDWARD SALK IS BORN.

Jonas Edward Salk was an American physician and medical researcher best known for the development of the first safe and effective polio vaccine. Salk did not seek wealth or fame through his innovations, famously stating, *'Who owns my polio vaccine? The people! Could you patent the Sun?'* In his later career, Salk devoted much energy toward the development of an AIDS vaccine.

29

1975 GENERAL FRANCO'S 36-YEAR REIGN ENDS.

General Franco's dictatorship of Spain effectively ended with the announcement that heir-designate Prince Juan Carlos would take over as provisional head of state. The move came as a result of the general's continuing illness following a series of heart attacks. Franco believed that Juan Carlos would continue at least the basic structure of his authoritarian regime. But after Franco's death in 1975, Juan Carlos began to dismantle the institutions of Franco's system and encouraged the revival of previously banned political parties. Within three years of Franco's death Spain had become a democratic constitutional monarchy, with a prosperous economy and democratic institutions similar to those of the rest of Western Europe.

1929 US stock market prices collapse on a day known as 'Black Tuesday', further fuelling the crisis known as the Great Depression.

30

1938 *WAR OF THE WORLDS* RADIO SHOW CAUSES NATIONAL PANIC.

A radio show was aired featuring a group of performers from New York's Mercury Theatre, most notably the young actor Orson Welles. The programme was based on H. G. Wells's *War of the Worlds* and the performance used the format of a news bulletin, announcing an attack on New Jersey by invaders from Mars. Thousands of listeners, not realising the announcement was a simulation, were panic-stricken. The event brought Orson Welles notoriety and instant fame and offers from Hollywood would soon follow, leading to a brilliant but often troubled career in American cinema.

31

1984 PRIME MINISTER INDIRA GANDHI IS ASSASSINATED.
Indira Gandhi was the only child of Jawaharlal Nehru, the first prime minister of independent India. She had served as prime minister of India for three consecutive terms (1966–77), and a fourth term (1980–84). She was assassinated on this day in 1984 by two of her own Sikh bodyguards. The murder was revenge for an army attack that Gandhi had authorised in June 1984 on the Golden Temple of Amritsar, the Sikhs' holiest shrine, which led to the deaths of more than 450 Sikhs.

1926 Harry Houdini, the magician and escape artist, dies of peritonitis stemming from a stomach injury.

November

1

1938 THE RACEHORSE SEABISCUIT WINS AGAINST THE FAVOURITE, WAR ADMIRAL, IN A RACE DESCRIBED AS 'THE MATCH OF THE CENTURY'.
As a three-year-old colt, Seabiscuit had lost every race he had ever entered. Temperamental, lazy and knobbly kneed, he was often the butt of stable jokes. However, when trainer Tom Smith took him in hand, the horse began to win. On 1 November 1938, Seabiscuit triumphed against the runaway favourite War Admiral in the Pimlico Special in Baltimore, Maryland. His unexpected success was a welcome diversion to millions of people during the Great Depression, and he became a national phenomenon, receiving more media coverage than such world leaders as Franklin Roosevelt and Adolf Hitler. In 2003, the movie *Seabiscuit*, which celebrated the horse's life, was nominated for seven Academy Awards.

1986 A catastrophic fire at a chemicals factory near Basel, Switzerland, sends tonnes of toxic chemicals into the nearby river Rhine and turns it red.

2

1917 BRITAIN SUPPORTS THE CREATION OF A JEWISH HOMELAND.
The British foreign secretary Arthur James Balfour declared the government's intention to establish a Jewish homeland in Palestine. The government hoped that this would help increase Jewish support for the Allied effort in the First World War. The Balfour Declaration was included in the British mandate over (control of) Palestine, and was approved by the League of Nations in 1922. Arabs opposed the Balfour Declaration, fearing that it would result in Jewish domination of Arab Palestinians. Jewish-Arab violence in the region became a recurring theme of twentieth century Middle Eastern politics.

1976 Democrat Jimmy Carter is elected 39th president of the United States.

3

1954 THE ARTIST HENRI MATISSE DIES IN NICE, FRANCE.
Henri Matisse, often regarded as the most important French painter of the twentieth century, died on 3 November 1954. He led the Fauvist movement of art around 1900 and pursued the expressiveness of colour throughout his career. The Fauves painted directly from nature, as the Impressionists had before them, but Fauvist works were invested with a strong expressive reaction to the subjects portrayed. Fauve artists

used pure, brilliant colour aggressively applied straight from the paint tubes to create a sense of an explosion on the canvas.

1957 The Soviet Union launches *Sputnik 2*; on board is the first living creature to enter orbit, a dog named Laika.

1970 Salvador Allende is inaugurated as president of Chile.

4

1995 YITZHAK RABIN IS ASSASSINATED.
While attending a peace rally, Israeli prime minister Yitzhak Rabin was assassinated in 1995 by a Jewish extremist. Rabin was an Israeli statesman and soldier who, as prime minister of Israel, had led his country towards peace with its Palestinian and Arab neighbours.

Rabin put a freeze on new Israeli settlements in the occupied territories and his government undertook secret negotiations with the Palestine Liberation Organisation (PLO) that led to the Israel-PLO accords of 1993. In these accords Israel recognised the PLO and agreed to implement limited self-rule for Palestinians in the West Bank and Gaza Strip. In October 1994, Rabin and King Hussein of Jordan signed a full peace treaty between their two countries. Rabin received the Nobel Prize for Peace in 1994, along with Shimon Peres, his foreign minister, and PLO chairman Yasir 'Arafat.

119

5

1913 THE MENTALLY ILL KING OTTO OF BAVARIA IS DEPOSED BY HIS COUSIN, PRINCE REGENT LUDWIG, WHO ASSUMES THE TITLE LUDWIG III.
The last king of Bavaria, Ludwig III became increasingly unpopular during the First World War because of his loyalty to Prussia. In 1918, towards the end of the war, a revolution broke out in Bavaria and Ludwig and his large family fled their palace in Munich. He was the first of the monarchs in the German Empire to be deposed. In November 1918 he signed a document releasing both civil and military officers from their oaths; the newly formed republican government of Kurt Eisner interpreted this as an abdication.

1935 Manufacturers Parker Brothers launch the board game Monopoly.

6

1962 THE UNITED NATIONS CONDEMNS APARTHEID.
The United Nations General Assembly adopted a resolution condemning South Africa's racist apartheid policies and calling on all member states to terminate economic and military relations with the country. After the 1960 massacre of unarmed demonstrators at Sharpeville near Johannesburg, South Africa, the

international movement to end apartheid gained wide international support. However, few major western powers, nor South Africa's other main trading powers, supported full economic or military sanctions against the country. Nonetheless, UN opposition grew, and in 1973 a UN resolution declared apartheid a crime against humanity.

7

1957 REPORT CALLS FOR MORE US MISSILES AND FALLOUT SHELTERS.
At the height of the Cold War, a report from a special government committee called to review the United States' defences indicated that the country was falling far behind the Soviets in missile capabilities. It said there was an urgent need to build fallout shelters to protect US citizens in the event of nuclear attack. The committee concluded that the United States was in danger of losing a war against the Soviets and demanded massive increases in the military budget. President Dwight D. Eisenhower had called for the committee to be formed following the stunning success of the Soviet *Sputnik I* in October 1957, but he seemed to be less than pleased with its findings.

8

1939 HITLER SURVIVES AN ASSASSINATION ATTEMPT.
On the sixteenth anniversary of Hitler's Munich (Beer Hall) Putsch, the German leader was the target of an assassination attempt. Hitler was addressing his followers in a beer hall in Munich and had finished his speech and left the podium. Minutes later a bomb exploded, killing eight people and wounding 65, among them Eva Braun's father. Hitler was unharmed. The man who had planted the bomb was believed to have been Johann Georg Elser, a cabinet-maker and critic of the Nazi regime. Elser was arrested, tortured by the Gestapo and eventually transported to Dachau concentration camp. He was executed by the SS two weeks before the end of the Second World War.

1974 The world famous fruit and vegetable market at Covent Garden in London closes after existing for more than 300 years.

9

1989 THE BERLIN WALL FALLS.
One of the most potent symbols of the Cold War, the Berlin Wall was opened up by the East German government. The Berlin Wall was erected in 1961 and eventually extended 45 km (28 miles) to divide the western and eastern sectors of Berlin. The original wall, built of barbed wire and cinder blocks, was subsequently replaced by a series of concrete walls (up to 5 m/16 ft high) that were topped with barbed wire and guarded with watchtowers, gun emplacements and mines. About 5,000 East Germans managed to cross the Berlin Wall and reach West Berlin safely, while another 5,000 were captured by East German authorities in the attempt and 191

more were killed attempting to climb the wall. On 9 November 1989, after 28 years, East Germans could at last travel freely to the West.

1938 The start of Kristallnacht ('Crystal Night' or 'Night of Broken Glass'), some 48 hours of Nazi-orchestrated anti-Jewish violence that erupts throughout Germany and Austria, resulting in the destruction and vandalising of synagogues and Jewish businesses, along with the deaths of at least 91 Jews. The name refers to the litter of broken glass left in the streets following the attacks.

10

1995 KEN SARO-WIWA IS EXECUTED IN NIGERIA.
The author and environmental activist Ken Saro-Wiwa, along with eight fellow activists from the Movement for the Survival of the Ogoni People (Mosop), was hanged by government forces in Nigeria. Saro-Wiwa had long spoken out against the Nigerian military regime and the Anglo-Dutch petroleum company Shell for causing environmental damage to the Ogoni People's lands in the Niger delta region. The executions aroused international condemnation and led to calls for economic sanctions against Nigeria and to its suspension from the Commonwealth.

11

1918 THE FIRST WORLD WAR ENDS.
At 5 a.m. on 11 November 1918, the Allied powers and Germany signed an armistice document in the railway carriage of Ferdinand Foch, the commander of the Allied armies. At 11 a.m. on the same day, the First World War came to an end. The casualties suffered during the First World War outstripped those of any previous war. Some 8.5 million soldiers had died as a result of wounds and/or disease. The greatest number of casualties and wounds were inflicted by artillery, followed by small arms, and then by poison gas. The heaviest loss of life for a single day occurred on 1 July 1916, during the Battle of the Somme, when the British army suffered 57,470 casualties.

1921 On the anniversary of the end of the First World War, the first Armistice Day is commemorated with the burial of the bodies of unknown soldiers in tombs in Paris, London and near Washington, D.C.

12

1990 EMPEROR AKIHITO IS ENTHRONED.
Japanese Emperor Akihito was formally enthroned nearly two years after the death of his father. Akihito was the fifth child and eldest son of Emperor Hirohito and Empress Nagako and, according to tradition, was the 125th direct descendant of Jimmu, Japan's legendary first emperor. In 1959 Akihito had broken a 1,500-year-old Japanese tradition when he married a commoner, Shoda Michiko, the daughter of a wealthy businessman. His reign was designated Heisei, or 'Achieving Peace'.

1954 New York's main immigration control centre, Ellis Island, shuts down after 62 years.

13

1985 ERUPTING VOLCANO KILLS THOUSANDS IN COLOMBIA, SOUTH AMERICA.
About 23,000 people were killed following a volcanic eruption in northern Colombia in the second most deadly eruption of the twentieth century. The worst affected place was Armero, the province of Tolima's second largest city, about 80 km (50 miles) from the Colombian capital, Bogota. The volcano Nevado del Ruiz, known locally as 'The Sleeping Lion', erupted during the night when most of the city's 27,000 residents were asleep in bed. A mudflow from the volcano engulfed the town as it rushed down the mountainside. Armero still lies beneath the hardened mudflow deposits, and the government has declared the site of the buried city to be 'holy ground'.

14

1965 A MAJOR BATTLE OF VIETNAM WAR TAKES PLACE AT LA DRANG VALLEY.

The first significant contact between US troops and North Vietnamese forces took place today at la Drang Valley when US forces fought a pitched battle with communists. US troops were flown in by helicopter and, in spite of fierce North Vietnamese resistance, senior American officials in Saigon ultimately declared the Battle of the la Drang Valley a great victory. However, the North Vietnamese learned a valuable lesson during the battle. They realised that if they kept their combat troops physically close to US positions, US troops could not use artillery or air strikes without risking injury to their own troops. This style of fighting became the North Vietnamese practice for the rest of the war.

15

1940 GERMANS BOMBS DESTROY THE CITY OF COVENTRY, UK.
The German Luftwaffe bombed Coventry in a massive raid lasting more than ten hours. Successive waves of enemy aircraft dropped bombs indiscriminately. One of the many buildings hit included the fourteenth-century cathedral, which was all but destroyed. Two days later King George VI visited Coventry to see the devastation. Between 380 and 554 people were killed and several hundred were injured in the bombing. After the end of the Second World War a new cathedral was built, designed by architect Basil Spence. It was consecrated on 25 May 1962 and now stands alongside the skeleton of the war-damaged ruin.

1988 The first Fairtrade label, Max Havelaar, is launched in the Netherlands.

16

1988 BENAZIR BHUTTO IS ELECTED AS PAKISTAN'S PRIME MINISTER.
Benazir Bhutto was elected prime minister of Pakistan and became the first woman in modern history to lead a Muslim country. She served as prime minister from 1988 to 1990 and again from 1993 to 1996. Bhutto failed to combat Pakistan's widespread poverty, governmental corruption and increasing crime. In August 1990 the president of Pakistan, Ghulam Ishaq Khan, dismissed her government on charges of corruption and called for new elections, in which Bhutto was defeated. However, in elections held in October 1993 she once again became head of a coalition government. Under renewed charges of corruption, economic mismanagement and a decline of law and order, her government was dismissed by President Farooq Leghari in November 1996. Bhutto was assassinated in 2007.

1932 New York City's Palace Theatre is converted to a cinema, marking the end of vaudeville (music hall) as a popular entertainment in the United States.

17

2003 ARNOLD SCHWARZENEGGER BECOMES GOVERNOR OF CALIFORNIA.
Republican Arnold Schwarzenegger, an Austrian-born American bodybuilder, film actor and six times Mr Universe winner, was inaugurated as the governor of California following a recall election that ousted the sitting governor. Schwarzenegger started acting in movies in 1970 and went on to make box-office hits such as *Conan the Barbarian* (1982), *The Terminator* (1984) and *Kindergarten Cop* (1990). He became a US citizen in 1983 and, during the 1990s became increasingly active in the Republican Party at both state and national levels.

18

1978 CULT MEMBERS DIE IN THE JONESTOWN MASSACRE.
Some 900 people, 276 of them children, were found dead in a compound belonging to the People's Temple Christian Church in Guyana, South America. Most of the dead had consumed a soft drink laced with cyanide and sedatives, others had died from gunshot wounds.

Jim Jones, leader of the People's Temple, attracted mostly African Americans to his religious community, with its vision of an integrated congregation. In 1974 Jones founded Jonestown, an agricultural settlement in San Francisco. In 1977 he led hundreds of the group's members to Guyana from San Francisco after an investigation began into the church for tax evasion. On 18 November 1978 the group took part in a mass rite of murder-suicide. The members of the group who had remained in San Francisco later formally disbanded.

1987 Church envoy Terry Waite is freed by the Islamic extremists who kidnapped him in Beirut.

19

1916 THE GOLDWYN COMPANY IS FORMED.
Samuel Goldwyn was born Schmuel Gelbfisz in Warsaw, Poland. When just a teenager he left Europe for the United States, arriving there penniless. Following a career as a glove salesman, and with his name anglicised to Samuel Goldfish, he found his way into the film business. In 1916 he formed a partnership with Edgar Selwyn and they called their company Goldwyn Pictures, a blend of their surnames. In 1918, Samuel Goldfish legally changed his surname to Goldwyn and eventually became one of the world's most successful independent film producers, owning his own studio and supporting his own stable of stars.

1994 The first National Lottery draw is held in Britain; a £1 ticket gives a one-in-14-million chance of correctly guessing the winning six out of 49 numbers.

20

1945 THE NUREMBERG WAR-CRIMES TRIALS BEGIN.
A series of trials of accused Nazi war criminals, conducted by a US, French, and Soviet military tribunal based in Nuremberg, Germany, began today. The indictment lodged against them contained four counts: 1) crimes against peace (i.e. the planning, initiating and waging of wars of aggression in violation of international treaties and agreements); 2) crimes against humanity (i.e. exterminations, deportations and genocide); 3) war crimes (i.e. violations of the laws of war); and 4) 'a common plan or conspiracy to commit' the criminal acts listed in the first three counts. Twenty-four former Nazi officials were tried, and when it was all over, one year later, half would be sentenced to death by hanging.

21

1980 WHO SHOT J. R.?
Episode 4, Season 4 of the long-running, prime-time drama series *Dallas* aired on US television. Examining the lives of a super-rich family of Texas oil barons, Dallas had already established a huge following. This episode, entitled 'Who Done It?', revealed the identity of the person behind the mystery shooting of J. R. Ewing (played by Larry Hagman), the show's scheming, womanising bad guy. It was one of the highest-rated episodes of a television show ever aired.

1995 *Toy Story* is released by Walt Disney Pictures. Produced by Pixar Animation Studios, it is the first feature-length film created completely using computer-generated imagery (CGI).

22

1963 US PRESIDENT JOHN F. KENNEDY IS ASSASSINATED.

The most notorious political murder in recent history occurred this day in 1963, when John F. Kennedy, the 35th US president, was shot and killed in Dallas, Texas, while riding in an open car.

With his wife Jacqueline sitting next to him, Kennedy was riding in a motorcade through Dealey Plaza in downtown Dallas. At 12.30 p.m. the president was hit by two rifle bullets, one at the base of his neck and one in the head. He was pronounced dead shortly after arrival at Parkland Memorial Hospital. Texas Governor John Connally, who had been riding in the front seat of the car, was also gravely wounded but he later recovered. Lee Harvey Oswald, a 24-year-old Dallas citizen, was accused of the shooting. Two days later Oswald was also shot to death in the basement of a Dallas police station.

23

1980 SOUTHERN ITALY IS ROCKED BY AN EARTHQUAKE

An earthquake in southern Italy killed more than 3,000 people. The tremor struck at 7.34 p.m. during Sunday night Mass, when many residents were sitting in church. Measuring 7.2 on the Richter scale, the earthquake centred on the town of Eboli, south of Naples. In nearby Balvano, children were preparing for their first communion at the 1,000-year-old church. The violent shaking demolished the church and killed scores of people, including 26 children.

Throughout southern Italy, fires broke out when gas lines ruptured. Much of the area's water supply was disrupted by broken piping, which meant that firefighting efforts were severely hampered. Extensive damage to the roads and railways leading into the small villages that dominated the region slowed down the rescue and relief efforts. To make matters even worse, a heavy fog blanketed the area that evening and the next morning.

1963 The first episode of the long-running science fiction television series *Doctor Who* airs on the BBC.

24

1963 LEE HARVEY OSWALD IS SHOT DEAD.

In Dallas, Texas, while being transferred from a jail cell to an interrogation office, Lee Harvey Oswald, the accused assassin of US president John F. Kennedy, was shot dead. The assassin, Dallas nightclub owner Jack Ruby, claimed he was acting out of rage and anguish over the death of the president. A special commission set up to investigate the assassination of President Kennedy (the Warren Commission) later concluded that Oswald alone had fired the shots killing Kennedy and that there was no evidence that either Oswald or Ruby had been part of any conspiracy. However, in January 1979, after a two-year investigation, a special US House of

Representatives Assassinations Committee reported that a second assassin may also have fired a shot and that there may have been a conspiracy. The mystery of who assassinated John F. Kennedy and why they did it persists to this day.

1965 The British government imposes an experimental 70 mph (113 km/h) speed limit on motorways.

25

1973 'HATED' GREEK PRESIDENT IS DEPOSED.

The Greek government was overthrown by the country's armed forces after weeks of unrest. There was little resistance when tanks rolled into Athens and troops took up positions around government buildings shortly before dawn.

The coup followed growing unrest in Greece, and came eight days after student uprisings in which 13 people died and hundreds were injured.

The former Greek leader and self-appointed president, George Papadopoulos, had come to power in a military coup six years earlier and his regime was characterised by repression and brutality. Papadopoulos was convicted of treason and sentenced to death by firing squad. This was later commuted to life in prison.

After a brief interim period, the exiled former prime minister Constantine Karamanlis was recalled to the country to head a new government. He was credited with guiding the country's return to democracy and engineering its entry into the European Economic Community in 1980.

1999 The United Nations General Assembly passes a resolution designating 25 November as the International Day for the Elimination of Violence Against Women to raise awareness of domestic abuse.

26

1924 THE MONGOLIAN PEOPLE'S REPUBLIC IS PROCLAIMED.

In 1919, following the unrest created by the Russian Revolution, a faction within the Chinese government sent a military expedition into Mongolia. The Chinese representatives forced the Mongols to sign a 'request' to be taken over by China. Almost immediately afterwards, defeated White Russian (anti-Bolshevik) troops from Russia began to enter Mongolia. Their most important leader was Baron Roman von Ungern-Sternberg, known as the 'Mad Baron', who defeated the Chinese occupation forces but then treated the Mongols with unfeeling savagery.

Some of the Mongols rose up in the form of a group of revolutionaries and asked the Bolsheviks for help, which was quickly granted. The Baron and the White Russians were defeated and the Mongolian People's Republic was proclaimed.

1933 In Paris, France, Camille Chautemps forms a government after former premier Albert Saurraut resigns.

27

1942 THE FRENCH SCUTTLE THEIR FLEET AT TOULON.
During the Second World War, the French admiral Jean de Laborde sank his own fleet anchored in Toulon harbour, off the southern coast of France, in order to keep it out of German hands. As the Germans launched Operation Lila – an attempt to commandeer the French fleet – Laborde ordered the sinking of two battle cruisers, four heavy cruisers, two light cruisers, one aircraft transport, 30 destroyers and 16 submarines. Three French submarines managed to escape the Germans and make it to Algiers, Allied territory in North Africa. Only one submarine fell into German hands. The Nazis' plan to gain a naval base in southern France had been thwarted.

1942 The birth of American guitarist Jimi Hendrix, who would change the course of pop music through his innovative playing of the electric guitar and his standing as a symbol of the 1960s' youth movement.

28

1990 PRIME MINISTER THATCHER STANDS DOWN.
Britain gained a new prime minister for the first time in more than 11 years. Conservative prime minister Margaret Thatcher formally tendered her resignation to the queen early in the morning after leaving Downing Street in London for the last time. The woman known as the 'Iron Lady' during her premiership made a tearful farewell speech from the doorstep of No. 10. John Major was elected to succeed Thatcher by Conservative Party members and he arrived at Downing Street a short while after her departure. Major served as prime minister until May 1997, when the Conservatives were ousted from power after a Labour Party landslide victory.

1919 Lady Nancy Astor becomes the first woman MP elected to the British House of Commons.

29

1947 THE UN VOTES IN FAVOUR OF THE PARTITION OF PALESTINE.
The United Nations voted to divide British-ruled Palestine into two states, one Jewish and the other Arab. Following the Second World War, Britain was under pressure to find a homeland for Jewish survivors of the Holocaust in Europe. The British government decided to end its mandate over Palestine because it was alarmed by the growing violence between Arabs and Jewish immigrants there. It handed the problem to the newly formed United Nations, which voted for partition. The Jewish people were to possess more than half of Palestine, even though they made up less than half of Palestine's population. Palestinian Arabs immediately opposed the decision.

30

1996 THE STONE OF SCONE RETURNS HOME AT LAST.

A rectangular block of sandstone known as the Stone of Scone, or Stone of Destiny, was returned to Scotland 700 years after King Edward I had taken it to England as war booty. For centuries the stone was associated with the crowning of Scottish kings and was kept in the seat of a royal coronation chair. John de Balliol was the last Scottish king to be crowned on it in 1292. Then in 1296 Edward I of England invaded Scotland and moved the stone to London.

At Westminster Abbey Edward had a special throne, called the Coronation Chair, built so that the stone fitted under it. This was to be a symbol that kings of England would also be crowned as kings of Scotland. On Christmas morning 1950, the stone was stolen from Westminster Abbey by Scottish nationalists who took it back to Scotland. Four months later it was recovered and restored to the abbey. In 1996 the British government returned the stone to Scotland.

1954 The first modern record of human injury caused by a missile from outer space occurs when a meteorite crashes through the roof of a house in Sylacauga, Alabama, USA, bounces off a radio and strikes a woman on the hip.

December

1

1959 THE ANTARCTIC TREATY IS SIGNED.
An agreement was signed by the nations of Argentina, Australia, Belgium, Britain, Chile, France, Japan, New Zealand, Norway, South Africa, the United States and the Soviet Union, in which the Antarctic continent was made a demilitarised zone to be preserved for scientific research. The treaty did not deny or support national claims to territorial sovereignty in Antarctica, but it did forbid all contracting parties from establishing military bases, carrying out military manoeuvres, testing any weapons (including nuclear weapons), or disposing of radioactive waste in the area. The treaty encouraged the freedom of scientific investigation and the exchange of scientific information and personnel in Antarctica.

2

1942 THE FIRST NUCLEAR CHAIN REACTION IS ACHIEVED.
The first controlled nuclear fission reaction took place in an unused squash court in a basement at the University of Chicago. The experiment was carried out by a team of scientists led by Italian physicist Enrico Fermi. In 1939, Fermi, along with Hungarian-born physicist Leo Szilard and German-born physicist Albert Einstein, had written to US President Franklin Roosevelt warning that the German Nazis were on the brink of developing an atomic bomb. The president acted on their warning and by 1942 the 'Manhattan Project' to build an atomic bomb was underway. In July 1945, the United States successfully tested the world's first atomic bomb, and in August US planes dropped two atomic bombs on Hiroshima and Nagasaki in Japan.

1966 In Britain, the symbol of the Swinging Sixties, the mini-skirt, is banned from the Houses of Parliament in London.

3

1967 THE FIRST SUCCESSFUL HEART TRANSPLANT IS CARRIED OUT.
Surgeon Christiaan Barnard performed the first successful heart transplant in Cape Town, South Africa. The patient was 53-year-old Lewis Washkansky, who received the transplant from Denise Darvall, a 25-year-old woman who had been fatally injured in a car accident. After the procedure, Washkansky was given drugs to suppress his immune system and keep his body from rejecting the heart. These drugs also left him susceptible to infection, though, and 18 days later he died from double

pneumonia. Despite the setback, Washkansky's new heart had functioned normally until his death. In the 1970s the development of better anti-rejection drugs made transplantation more viable.

1926 British crime writer Agatha Christie disappears from her home in Surrey. She is found 11 days later staying under an assumed name at a hotel at Harrogate in Yorkshire.

4

1992 US PRESIDENT GEORGE BUSH ORDERS TROOPS TO SOMALIA, EAST AFRICA.
Towards the end of 1992, civil war, drought and clan-based fighting created famine conditions that threatened a quarter of Somalia's population with starvation. The United Nations began a humanitarian mission but found it difficult to distribute food because of the fighting, so the United States agreed to help with military aid. On 4 December, President George Bush sent 25,000 US troops to Somalia.

In June 1993, soldiers under Somali warlord General Mohammed Aidid killed 24 Pakistani UN peacekeepers. The US sent 400 elite troops in to capture Aidid, but they failed. On 3 October, 18 US soldiers were killed and 84 wounded in combat. Around 1,000 Somalis were killed in a violent 17-hour firefight. Three days later, with Aidid still at large, the new US president, Bill Clinton, ordered a complete US withdrawal. Devastating clan fighting continued in Somalia into the next century.

1937 One of Britain's best-loved comics, the *Dandy*, is first published by DC Thompson.

5

1933 PROHIBITION ENDS IN AMERICA.
In early 1919, a law was passed banning the manufacture, sale and transportation of intoxicating liquors within the United States. The ban led to bootlegging (the illegal distribution of alcohol, often illicitly distilled), to the financial advantage of organised crime. Speakeasies ('secret' clubs) for illicit drinking sprang up, and organised crime activity increased, especially in Chicago and towns near the Canadian border, led by notorious gangsters such as Al Capone. The public had little faith in the effectiveness of Prohibition and it officially ended on 5 December 1933.

6

1921 THE IRISH FREE STATE IS ESTABLISHED.
The Irish Free State, comprising four-fifths of Ireland but excluding Northern Ireland, was established, ending a five-year Irish struggle for independence from Britain. In

the Anglo-Irish Treaty of 6 December it was agreed that Ireland would remain part of the British Commonwealth, symbolically subject to the British monarch. A constitution adopted by the people in 1937 declared Ireland to be a sovereign, independent, democratic state, and the Irish Free State was renamed Éire.

The Republic of Éire remained neutral during the Second World War, and in 1949 the Republic of Ireland Act severed the last remaining link with the Commonwealth. Conflicts persisted over Northern Ireland, however, and the Irish Republican Army (IRA), outlawed in the south, fought to try to regain the six northern counties still ruled by Britain.

7

1941 THE JAPANESE MILITARY BOMBS PEARL HARBOR IN HAWAII, USA.

On the morning of Sunday, 7 December 1941, US neutrality in the Second World War ended when Japanese forces carried out a surprise attack on the US naval base Pearl Harbor on Oahu Island, Hawaii. Over 400 planes from six Japanese aircraft carriers bombed the harbour and airfield, and within two hours much of the US Pacific Fleet was rendered useless. Losses were devastating: five out of eight battleships, three destroyers and seven other ships were sunk or severely damaged, and more than half the island's aircraft were destroyed.

Fortunately for the United States, all three US Pacific Fleet carriers were out at sea at the time of the attack. A total of 2,300 Americans were killed and 1,200 were wounded that day, though. Japan's losses were 29 planes and five midget submarines. President Franklin D. Roosevelt described Pearl Harbor as the 'date which will live in infamy', and US public support for neutrality melted away. The next day, Japan attacked the Philippines, Malaya, Thailand and Hong Kong, while Britain and the United States declared war on Japan.

131

8

1980 JOHN LENNON IS SHOT.

Former Beatle John Lennon was shot and killed by an obsessed fan outside his luxury apartment in the Dakota Building in New York City. The 40-year-old Lennon was shot four times in the back by Mark Chapman, who had asked for his autograph only hours earlier. Chapman pleaded guilty to the murder, saying he had heard voices in his head telling him to kill the world-famous musician. Bereaved Lennon fans kept vigil in front of the entrance to his home for an entire week.

Lennon's wife, Yoko Ono, was with him on the night he died. She and Lennon had emphasised love and peace in their work. Earlier on in his career Lennon had caused outrage when he declared that the Beatles were more popular than Jesus.

Twenty years after his death, millions of fans paid tribute to Lennon in his home town of Liverpool, UK, and in New York. Yoko Ono launched a campaign against gun violence in the United States to mark the anniversary.

9

1987 INTIFADA (UPRISING) BEGINS ON THE GAZA STRIP.

The first riots of the Palestinian intifada (which means 'shaking' in Arabic) began on the Gaza Strip. This piece of land had been occupied by Israel since the Six-Day War of 1967. The uprising soon spread to the Israeli-occupied West Bank (captured from Jordan, also in 1967) and Palestinian demonstrators marched while youths threw stones at Israeli police, troops and citizens. Palestinian leaders called for the creation of an independent Palestine, and terrorist attacks against Israel increased.

Israel used force to combat the intifada, and arrested and deported thousands. In 1993, Palestine Liberation Organisation (PLO) Chairman Yasser Arafat drastically changed course and acknowledged the right of Israel to coexist with Palestine. Later that year, Arafat signed a peace accord with Israeli prime minister Yitzhak Rabin and a major peace agreement in 1994. In 2000, the peace process stalled and Palestinian-Israeli violence resumed.

1941 China declares war on the Axis powers: Japan, Germany and Italy.

10

1981 A MYSTERY EPIDEMIC KILLS HOMOSEXUALS.

A mysterious disease was discovered in homosexual men, and by 1981 was believed to have claimed around 75 lives. The unknown condition had been found in 180 patients in 15 US states since the previous July. It was eventually named as the AIDS (Acquired Immune Deficiency Syndrome) virus.

The disease caused widespread panic in the United States, where 4,000 people were infected in the space of two years. During that time it also became clear that the epidemic was not restricted to homosexuals. Cases of AIDS were also discovered among heterosexuals, drug users and blood-transfusion patients.

The virus that was isolated as the cause of the disease was called Human Immunodeficiency Virus (HIV) and was first discovered in 1983.

Around 24 million people have died from AIDS since it first emerged and it is the leading cause of death in sub-Saharan Africa.

1945 In London, the new Waterloo Bridge across the River Thames is opened; the bridge is designed by architect Sir Giles Gilbert Scott.

11

1936 EDWARD VIII ANNOUNCES HIS ABDICATION.

After ruling for less than one year, Edward VIII became the first English monarch to abdicate the throne voluntarily. The eldest son of King George V, Edward ascended to the throne in January 1936. His screen-idol looks made him very popular with the public until he announced his intention to marry Wallis Warfield Simpson, an

American divorcee. Many British people opposed the marriage, but the king refused to call off his engagement.

With no compromise possible, Edward announced his abdication. In a radio broadcast to the British people, he said:

'I have found it impossible to carry the heavy burden of responsibility and to discharge the duties of king, as I would wish to do, without the help and support of the woman I love.'

That evening, parliament passed a bill of abdication, and the next day Edward's younger brother was proclaimed King George VI. The former king was granted the title of Duke of Windsor and in 1937 he married Wallis Simpson in France.

12

2000 GEORGE W. BUSH WINS THE US PRESIDENTIAL ELECTION.
In one of the closest and most controversial elections in American history, George W. Bush became the first person since 1888 to become president, despite having lost the nationwide popular vote. Towards the end of the election campaign, the fight for the presidency between Republican Bush and Democrat Al Gore hinged on votes in the state of Florida.

After lengthy legal wrangling between the two political camps, the Florida Supreme Court decided to order a recount of the approximately 45,000 'undervotes' (i.e., ballots that vote-counting machines had recorded as not clearly expressing a presidential vote). The Bush camp quickly asked the US Supreme Court to delay the recounts until it could hear the case; a stay was issued by the court on 9 December. Three days later, concluding that a fair statewide recount could not be performed in time to meet the 18 December deadline for certifying the state's electors, the US Supreme Court reversed the Florida Supreme Court's recount order, effectively awarding the presidency to Bush.

133

1925 The world's first motel opens in California, USA.

13

1937 THE NANKING MASSACRE.
The Japanese Imperial Army seized the Chinese capital city of Nanking during the Sino-Japanese War. To break the spirit of Chinese resistance, Japanese General Matsui Iwane ordered that the city of Nanking be destroyed. Much of the city was burned, and Japanese troops launched a campaign of atrocities against civilians. In what became known as the 'Rape of Nanking', the Japanese butchered an estimated 150,000 male war prisoners, massacred an additional 50,000 male civilians, and raped at least 20,000 women and girls of all ages. Shortly after the end of the Second World War, Matsui was found guilty of war crimes by the International Military Tribunal for the Far East and executed.

1930 Prima ballerina Anna Pavlova makes her final public appearance.

14

1911 ROALD AMUNDSEN REACHES THE SOUTH POLE.
Norwegian Roald Amundsen became the first explorer to reach the South Pole. In early 1911, he had sailed his ship into Antarctica's Bay of Whales and set up base camp 62 miles (100 km) closer to the pole than British Captain Robert Falcon Scott, who was heading a rival expedition.

In October, both explorers set off – Amundsen using sleigh dogs and Scott employing Siberian motor sledges, ponies and dogs. On 14 December 1911, Amundsen's expedition won the race to the pole and returned safely to base camp in late January. Scott's team, on the other hand, encountered numerous problems and arrived at the Pole a month after Amundsen. Weather on the return journey was terrible – two members perished – and a storm later trapped Scott and the other two survivors in their tent only 18 km (11 miles) from their base camp. Scott's frozen body was found later that year.

1995 The Dayton Peace Accord ends three-year war in the Balkans.

15

1939 PREMIERE OF *GONE WITH THE WIND*
After an unprecedented period of advance promotion, including a highly publicised search for an actress to play the leading role, the film of Margaret Mitchell's 1936 novel, *Gone With the Wind*, premiered in Atlanta, Georgia. Starring Vivien Leigh as Scarlett O'Hara and Clark Gable as Rhett Butler, this romantic tale of the American South during the Civil War made box-office history. For 20 years it was the top money-making film of all time and it won eight major Oscars and two special Oscars at the Academy Awards.

1966 Cartoon film producer and showman Walt Disney dies in Los Angeles, USA.

16

1944 THE BATTLE OF THE BULGE BEGINS.
In the last German offensive on the Western Front in the Second World War, Adolf Hitler ordered a surprise attack on the Allied forces. The German counter-offensive out of the densely wooded Ardennes region in southern Belgium took the Allies by surprise and created a bulge 97 km (60 miles) deep into the front. As bad weather hampered the Allied aircraft, for several days Hitler's desperate gamble seemed to be paying off. However, the Allies kept up a fierce resistance, and on 23 December the skies cleared over the bulge. By January, the Germans had been pushed back to their original line, having lost some 120,000 men in the offensive.

17

1992 THE NORTH AMERICAN FREE TRADE AGREEMENT (NAFTA) IS SIGNED.
A trade pact signed on 17 December 1992 gradually eliminated most tariffs and other trade barriers on products and services passing between the United States, Canada and Mexico. The pact effectively created a free-trade bloc among the three largest countries of North America. NAFTA ensured eventual duty-free access for a vast range of manufactured goods and commodities traded between the signatories. Other provisions were designed to give US and Canadian companies greater access to Mexican markets in banking, insurance, advertising, telecommunications and trucking.

1967 British yachtsman Alec Rose arrives in Australia aboard his boat *The Lively Lady* after sailing solo from Britain – a voyage of 23,335 km (14,500 miles).

18

1916 THE BATTLE OF VERDUN ENDS.
The Battle of Verdun, the longest engagement of the First World War, ended after ten months and massive loss of life. In February 1916, German forces launched an offensive against Verdun, a city 220 km (137 miles) east of Paris. Initially the Germans advanced with little opposition, but the French rallied under General Henri Pétain, and a bloody stalemate ensued.

135

   On 1 July, a major British offensive in the Somme River region relieved some of the pressure on Verdun, as did the Russian offensive on the Eastern Front. By mid-December, the French had recovered most of the ground lost in the early days of the battle. When the Battle of Verdun ended with a French victory on 18 December, 23 million shells had been fired and 650,000 lives lost.

19

1946 THE FIRST INDOCHINA WAR BEGINS.
On 19 December 1946, 30,000 Vietnamese soldiers under their leader Ho Chi Minh attacked French positions in Hanoi, Vietnam. Ho Chi Minh had first travelled to France at the end of the First World War to press for Vietnamese independence from the French. He also wanted a communist revolution. In 1945 Ho proclaimed the Democratic Republic of Vietnam, hoping to prevent the French from reclaiming their former colonial possession. Diplomatic efforts to gain independence collapsed, and French warships bombarded the North Vietnamese city of Haiphong in November 1946. Almost 6,000 Vietnamese people were killed.
   On 19 December, the Vietnamese launched the attack against the French in Hanoi, starting the First Indochina War. Eight years later, an armistice was signed, in which

Vietnam was divided into northern and southern regions, with Ho in command of the north and Emperor Bao Dai in control of the south pending free elections. In 1975, at the end of the Second Indochina War, Vietnam was united under communist rule.

1972 The US spacecraft *Apollo 17* splashes down on target in the Pacific Ocean bringing an end the US *Apollo* programme of landing men on the Moon.

20

1989 THE USA INVADES PANAMA.

The United States invaded Panama in Central America in an attempt to overthrow its military dictator, Manuel Noriega. The US government had originally supported Noriega because of his anti-communist beliefs but, as Communism collapsed in Europe, the United States began to feel that it was no longer as important to give unqualified support to anti-communist regimes.

In the attack, the US invaders promptly crushed Noriega's Panamanian Defence Forces, and the dictator himself sought asylum in the Vatican embassy in Panama City. He surrendered in January and was taken to the USA, where he was indicted on drug trafficking charges and accused of suppressing democracy and endangering US nationals. Noriega was found guilty of drug trafficking and sentenced to 40 years in prison.

1957 American rock 'n' roll star Elvis Presley is called up to join the US Army.

21

1988 TERRORISTS BLOW UP PANAM FLIGHT 103 OVER THE SCOTTISH TOWN OF LOCKERBIE.

In the Lockerbie disaster, a terrorist bomb exploded on board a PanAm jumbo jet carrying 259 passengers and crew. All on board were killed, as were 11 people in the town where the plane crashed. The plane was bound for New York and exploded 38 minutes after take-off from London's Heathrow airport. The subsequent police investigation was the biggest ever mounted in Scotland and became a murder inquiry when evidence of a bomb was found. Two men accused of being Libyan intelligence agents were eventually charged with planting the bomb.

1937 Walt Disney's first full-length colour animated cartoon *Snow White and the Seven Dwarfs* premieres in Los Angeles, USA.

22

1989 THE ROMANIAN GOVERNMENT FALLS.

On 17 December 1989, Romanian leader Nicolae Ceausescu ordered his security forces to fire on anti-government demonstrators in the city of Timisoara. The demonstrations spread to Bucharest, and on 22 December the Romanian Army defected to the demonstrators. Ceausescu's government was overthrown; he and his wife fled from Bucharest in a helicopter, but were captured and convicted of mass murder in a hasty military trial. On 25 December they were executed by firing squad.

Ceausescu, ruler of Romania since 1965, had resisted the liberalisation of the USSR and other Soviet bloc countries in the late 1980s. By the time of his government's downfall in 1989, Romania was the most repressive and economically backward country in Europe.

1938 A fish, identified as a coelcanth – thought to have been extinct for 65 million years – is caught by a fisherman off the coast of South Africa.

23

1986 *VOYAGER* COMPLETES ITS GLOBAL FLIGHT

Voyager became the first aircraft to fly around the world without stops or refuelling. Piloted by Americans Richard Rutan and Jeana Yeager, the experimental plane circled the globe in nine days, three minutes and 44 seconds. *Voyager*'s extremely light but strong body was made mostly of plastic, and its weight decreased by 80 per cent as fuel was consumed. On 23 December 1986, *Voyager* returned to its starting point at Edwards Air Force Base in California after travelling 40,251 km (25,011 miles).

1940 At the height of the Second World War, British prime minister Winston Churchill urges the Italians to rid themselves of dictator Benito Mussolini.

24

1968 ASTRONAUTS ORBIT THE MOON.

US space capsule *Apollo 8*, the first manned mission to the Moon, entered lunar orbit on 24 December 1968. During the *Apollo*'s ten orbits of the Moon, television images and spectacular photos were taken of Earth and the Moon. American astronauts Frank Borman, James Lovell and William Anders became the first humans ever to see the dark side of the Moon.

On Christmas morning, *Apollo 8* left its lunar orbit and began its journey back to Earth, landing safely in the Pacific Ocean on 27 December. On 20 July the following year, Neil Armstrong and Buzz Aldrin, astronauts of the *Apollo 11* mission, became the first men to walk on the Moon.

25

1926 EMPEROR HIROHITO IS CROWNED IN JAPAN.

Following the death of his father, Michinomiya Hirohito was enthroned as the 124th Japanese monarch in an imperial line dating back to 660 BC. Emperor Hirohito presided over one of the most turbulent eras in his nation's history. From rapid military expansion beginning in 1931 to the crushing defeat of Japan by Allied forces in 1945, Hirohito ruled the Japanese people as an absolute monarch.

After US atomic bombs destroyed the Japanese cities of Hiroshima and Nagasaki, Hirohito argued for his country's surrender, explaining to the Japanese people in his first-ever radio address that the unendurable must be endured. Under US occupation and post-war reconstruction, Hirohito was formally stripped of his powers and forced to renounce his alleged divinity, but he remained his country's official figurehead until his death in 1989. He was the longest-reigning monarch in Japanese history.

1974 The town of Darwin in Australia is devastated by a cyclone.

26

1908 JACK JOHNSON WINS THE HEAVYWEIGHT BOXING TITLE.
Jack Johnson was the first African American to win the world heavyweight title when he knocked out Canadian champion Tommy Burns in Sydney, Australia. Johnson received little support in the United States, where many called for a 'Great White Hope' to regain the heavyweight title for white men. Johnson defeated several US challengers and successfully defended his international title.

Johnson's two marriages to white women further infuriated American racists. In 1912 he was convicted of violating an old US law forbidding a man from transporting an unmarried woman across state lines. He was sentenced to a year in prison, but fled to Europe and was a fugitive for seven years. In 1915 he lost a fight to white American Jess Willard in Cuba.

In 1920 he returned to the United States and was imprisoned for a year. After his release, he boxed occasionally and became a vaudeville and carnival performer, appearing finally with a trained flea act. He died in a car accident in 1946.

2004 A massive tsunami in Southeast Asia claims around 230,000 lives.

27

1979 SOVIETS OVERTHROW THE GOVERNMENT IN AFGHANISTAN.
Soviet troops invaded Afghanistan and overthrew the government of President Hafizullah Amin, murdering him in the process. They installed Afghan politician Babrak Karmal in his place. Despite early gains, the Soviet Army had reckoned without the resistance of Muslim guerrillas, who launched a jihad, or holy war, against the foreigners. Armed by the United States, Britain, China and several Muslim nations, the *mujahideen*, or holy warriors, inflicted heavy casualties on the Soviets. In April 1988, after years of stalemate, Soviet leader Mikhail Gorbachev signed a peace accord with Afghanistan. The last Soviet soldier left Afghanistan in 1989.

1927 Russian revolutionary Leon Trotsky is expelled from the Communist Party.

28

1957 FOOT-AND-MOUTH SHUTS DOWN ABATTOIR.

The biggest abattoir in the north of England was shut down after foot-and-mouth disease was found in cattle waiting to be slaughtered. The Stanley abattoir in Liverpool supplied meat to areas throughout the north-west, and thousands of animals were usually slaughtered there each week.

The 1956–58 outbreak of foot-and-mouth disease reached its peak in 1957 and affected 20 counties in England and Wales. More than 30,000 animals were slaughtered in an attempt to contain the disease. In 2001, foot-and-mouth struck again, and on a scale which dwarfed earlier outbreaks. Over 2,000 cases were reported, and an estimated four million animals were slaughtered across the UK.

1975 An underground explosion at a coal mine in north-east India claims the lives of 372 men.

1942 During the Second World War, Japanese planes bomb Calcutta in India.

29

1940 THE BLITZ ON LONDON.

On the evening of 29 December 1940, London suffered its most devastating air raid when German aircraft firebombed the city. Hundreds of fires caused by the exploding bombs engulfed areas of London, but firefighters battling the inferno succeeded in saving much of the city from destruction. The next day, a newspaper photo of St Paul's Cathedral standing undamaged amid the smoke and flames seemed to symbolise the capital's unconquerable spirit during the Battle of Britain.

1950 Radio Luxembourg begins broadcasting in Europe.

30

1916 RUSSIAN 'HOLY MAN' RASPUTIN IS MURDERED.

Grigory Rasputin, adviser to the Russian royal family, was murdered by nobles eager to end his reign of power. Rasputin had won the favour of Tsar Nicholas II and his wife Alexandra through his ability to stop the bleeding of their haemophiliac son, Alexei. While the Siberian-born peasant was widely criticised for his womanising and drunkenness, he exerted a powerful influence over Alexandra. When Nicholas departed to lead Russian forces in the First World War, Rasputin effectively ruled Russia through her.

In the early hours of 30 December 1916, a group of Russian nobles lured Rasputin to Yusupovsky Palace, where they attempted to poison him. Rasputin survived the large doses of poison placed in his wine and food. The nobles then shot him at close range and he collapsed but then rose, beat one of his assailants, and attempted to escape from the palace grounds, where he was shot again. Rasputin, still alive, was then bound and tossed into a freezing river. A few months later, the monarchy was overthrown by the Russian Revolution.

31

1911 MARIE CURIE AWARDED NOBEL PRIZE FOR CHEMISTRY.

On 31 December 1911, the scientist Marie Curie received a second Nobel Prize – an unprecedented event in the history of the award. Born in Poland, Curie had won her first Nobel Prize along with her husband, French scientist Pierre Curie, and fellow scientist Henri Becquerel in 1903. She was the first woman to win a Nobel Prize.

Marie and Pierre discovered the radioactive element polonium (so-called by Marie in honour of her native land) in the summer of 1898, and the element radium a few months later. The 1903 Nobel Prize for Physics was awarded to the three scientists for the discovery of radioactivity.

Index

142